Cambridge Elements ≡

Elements in Environmental Humanities
edited by
Louise Westling
University of Oregon
Serenella Iovino
University of North Carolina at Chapel Hill
Timo Maran
University of Tartu

WASTEOCENE

Stories from the Global Dump

Marco Armiero

KTH Royal Institute of Technology, Sweden/Consiglio Nazionale delle Ricerche, Italy

CAMBRIDGE
UNIVERSITY PRESS

CAMBRIDGE
UNIVERSITY PRESS

University Printing House, Cambridge CB2 8BS, United Kingdom

One Liberty Plaza, 20th Floor, New York, NY 10006, USA

477 Williamstown Road, Port Melbourne, VIC 3207, Australia

314–321, 3rd Floor, Plot 3, Splendor Forum, Jasola District Centre,
New Delhi – 110025, India

79 Anson Road, #06–04/06, Singapore 079906

Cambridge University Press is part of the University of Cambridge.

It furthers the University's mission by disseminating knowledge in the pursuit of
education, learning, and research at the highest international levels of excellence.

www.cambridge.org
Information on this title: www.cambridge.org/9781108826747
DOI: 10.1017/9781108920322

First published 2021

A catalogue record for this publication is available from the British Library.

ISBN 978-1-108-82674-7 Paperback
ISSN 2632-3125 (online)
ISSN 2632-3117 (print)

Wasteocene

Stories from the Global Dump

Elements in Environmental Humanities

DOI: 10.1017/9781108920322
First published online: April 2021

Marco Armiero
KTH Royal Institute of Technology, Sweden/Consiglio Nazionale delle Ricerche, Italy

Author for correspondence: Marco Armiero, armiero@kth.se

Abstract: Humans may live in the Anthropocene, but this does not affect all in the same way. How would the Anthropocene look if, instead of searching its traces in the geosphere, researchers would look for them in the organosphere, in the ecologies of humans in their entanglements with the environment? Looking at this embodied stratigraphy of power and toxicity, more than the Anthropocene, we will discover the Wasteocene. The imposition of wasting relationships on subaltern human and more-than-human communities implies the construction of toxic ecologies made of contaminating substances and narratives. While official accounts have systematically erased any trace of those wasting relationships, another kind of narrative has been written in flesh, blood, and cells. Traveling between Naples (Italy) and Agbogbloshie (Ghana), science fiction and epidemic outbreaks, this Element will take the readers into the bowels of the Wasteocene, but it will also indicate the commoning practices which are dismantling it.

Keywords: anthropocene, capitalism, commoning, toxicity, waste

ISBNs: 9781108826747 (PB), 9781108920322 (OC)
ISSNs: 2632-3125 (online), 2632-3117 (print)

Contents

1 Introduction

Growing up in Naples, Italy, in the 1970s, I had a schoolmate in primary school who would always fall asleep in class because he had been up all night "making cardboard" (*facendo i cartoni*, in the Neapolitan dialect). However, "making" is not exactly the correct term. Salvatore, along with many other Neapolitan children at the time, was not working in a paper factory "making" cardboard; rather, they spent the night collecting them from piles of urban rubbish, riding through the city on the back of the characteristic Italian three-wheeled commercial vehicle known as the Apecar. This activity was so common in the city at the time that the Neapolitan folk singer Pino Daniele included the *cartonaio* – we could translate this as the waste picker – as an iconic figure in his poetic description of the city night. Indeed, those were workers in a different kind of factory, the metropolis, where production and consumption are less separated than one might assume; thereby, one could "make" things by recovering them from the open veins of the urban mine.

This autobiographical note contains some of the main issues that are inherent to the most recent scholarship on waste, including the very meaning of waste (what is waste and for whom), the metabolic relationship of work and waste, the urban dimension of waste, and the controversy over waste ownership. The fact that at a certain point Salvatore disappeared from my classroom, leaving school for good, while I became a professor, illustrates that waste is not considered here as a thing, but rather as a set of socio-ecological relationships aiming to (re) produce exclusion and inequalities.

Ironically, writing about waste is a mess in itself. The amount of scholarship accumulated over this topic and its diversity in terms of disciplines and approaches is almost unbelievable. From anthropology to history, from ecocriticism to sociology, passing through economics, law, political science, geography, archeology, design, philosophy and many more disciplines I am now forgetting (shame on me!), waste is an extremely hot topic. This Element is not conceived as a long literature review on waste, partially because it will be incomplete and almost immediately outdated, but even more because I have designed it with a different aim. This Element is meant to propose the Wasteocene, that is, a narrative linking waste, justice, and the making of our present world. The Wasteocene is, evidently, in dialogue with the explosion of academic and arts debates and events around the Anthropocene. The Wasteocene can be enlisted among the creative alternatives to the Anthropocene which have bloomed especially among environmental humanities scholars who were unsatisfied with the overly neutral flavor of the "Age of Humans" (Malm & Hornborg 2014). Capitalocene has gained terrain for its

direct reference to the economic and social system that many consider responsible for the current socio-ecological crisis (Moore 2016). The Wasteocene
assumes that waste can be considered the planetary mark of our new epoch.
However, this is not solely because of its ubiquitous presence – after all, even
CO_2 emissions are basically atmospheric waste – rather, I argue that what makes
the Wasteocene are the wasting relationships, those really planetary in their
scope, which produce wasted people and places.[1]

If waste is not a thing to be placed somewhere but a set of wasting relationships producing wasted human and nonhuman beings, then wasted places, and
wasted stories, the proximity, or overlapping, of a given community and
a contaminating facility is more than a matter of miles and ZIP codes. Waste
as a relation (wasting) *produces* the targeted community rather than solely
selecting it as the ideal place for an unwanted facility. In this sense, we might
adapt what Dipesh Chakrabarty once wrote on the issue of waste:

> For whether we are talking about radioactive waste from the industrialised
> countries or of the waste of a household or village in India, the "dirt" can only
> go to a place that is designated as the "outside." (Chakrabarty 1992, 542)

The practice of "othering," which is inherent to the colonial project, rests at the
heart of any wasting relationship. The production of waste is connected to the
production of the other, or the outside, and of the "us." As Gay Hawkins has
argued, wasting does not only define who the Others are, but also "who we are"
(Hawkins 2006, 2). The Wasteocene is to coloniality what the Anthropocene is
to the species discourse – now so cherished by Chakrabarty (2009). We might
say that "othering," that is, the colonial production of the other, and "saming,"
that is, the rhetorical invention of the "us," are two sides of the same coin.[2] The
othering produced through wasting is more pervasive than the making of
sacrifice zones. Othering means to change the "nature" of the other while
simultaneously using it to preserve a privilege.

In this Element I will illustrate how – perhaps I should say where – the
Wasteocene manifests itself. I will trace the histories of the Anthropocene
discourse (2.1) and propose the Wasteocene as an alternative framing for the
socio-ecological crisis (2.2). Then I will explore the science-fiction narratives of
the Wasteocene and how those imaginaries shape our ideas of the waste
apocalypse (2.3). I will uncover the wasting of toxic stories through obliteration
and domestication of memories or the imposition of mainstream narratives

---

[1] Here, I am building upon Bauman (2007) and his concept of "wasted humans."

[2] Although rich and ramified, the genealogy of the "othering" as the pillar of the imperial project
producing both the colonial other and the reassuring "we" of the colonizers has generally led to
the work of postcolonial theorist Gayatri Spivak.

which either blame the victims or naturalize injustice (3.1 and 3.2). The Wasteocene is both planetary and place-based; I will jump between these scales, illustrating through a series of brief vignettes the diverse manifestations of the wasting relationships in the United States, Brazil, and Ghana (3.3). In section 4, I will examine the Wasteocene through the microscope lens, employing Naples (Italy) as an in-depth case study. I will look at how some epiphanies in the history of the city – cholera epidemics, the "dark disease" in the 1970s, and the 1990s-2000s waste crisis – have opened breaches in the Wasteocene wall that divide those who are worthy from the "others." Section 5 is dedicated to the forces that within the Wasteocene are fighting to sabotage the wasting relationships and experimenting with new socio-ecological relationships. I will argue that commoning practices – that is, the collective practices generating commons (De Angelis 2017; Bollier & Helfrich 2012) – are the most generative anti-wasting strategies because as much as wasting relationships produce profit from exploitation and othering, commoning relationships, instead, produce well-being through care and inclusion. A few examples from COVID-19 solidarity brigades, waste pickers' associations in Brazil, and working-class communities from Catalonia, Bosnia-Herzegovina, and Italy will give flesh, blood, and dreams to this discourse.

Cambridge University Press Elements are, by design, short contributions which should deliver a clear message and, hopefully, spark discussion and foster further, perhaps deeper, research. Rereading my manuscript, I realize that many things are missing, and yet it could not have been otherwise. Although my interpretation assumes that wasting relationships affect both humans and nonhumans, in my writing I still maintain a quite anthropocentric focus. Nonetheless, I also make clear that as the Wasteocene logic reproduces wasted people and ecosystems, any alternative project cannot be anything less than a multispecies liberation alliance. My best hope is that this Element might inspire other scholars to create a better and more inclusive understanding of the Wasteocene, beyond the limitations of my approach.

2 From the Anthropocene to the Wasteocene

2.1 Return to Cuernavaca

Perhaps it is my social/professional bubble, but it seems to me that the Anthropocene is everywhere – at dinner with friends, on social media, at conferences, and on the shelves of any bookstore you walk into. There is no single day – at least in my life – without someone mentioning the Anthropocene. Rarely has a scientific concept become so popular. Google informs me that today (January 23, 2020) the word Anthropocene gives more than five million results in 0.7 minutes. The increasing currency of this concept goes hand in hand with the spreading anxiety about climate change. Given its popularity, it might be redundant to spend more words to explain it; nonetheless, I do feel that we need to start our journey to the Wasteocene from the Anthropocene, the ancestor of a myriad of "-cenes" born within and against it.

As every foundational narrative, also that of the Anthropocene can be quite difficult to track back. Perhaps, the easiest point of departure would be in Cuernavaca, a town not far away from Mexico City. However, this time it would not be a story of conquistadores but of scientists. It was in Cuernavaca that in 2000, during a conference, the Nobel laureate Paul Crutzen felt the urgency to announce that the Holocene had ended, and a new epoch had started. Will Steffen, an earth-system scientist who would soon become a crucial figure in the Anthropocene debate, has often told the story of how Crutzen paused for a moment before coming up with the term Anthropocene. Almost a revelation, one might say. That of Crutzen was, at that time, only an intuition, yet the message was instantly clear: humans should be seen as a geological force able to affect the entire planet. Nobody better than he could understand the planetary systemic consequences of human activities. Indeed, in 1995, Crutzen, together with Mario J. Molina and F. Sherwood Rowland, had won the Nobel Prize for Chemistry for their research on the depletion in the ozone layer caused by human-made emissions. The story of the discovery and remediation of the hole in the ozone layer was, without a doubt, the foundation for Crutzen's (re) invention of the Anthropocene. "Reinvention" because the story of the Cuernavaca conference and Crutzen's enlightening comment is, indeed, only one of the multiple origin stories of the Anthropocene. Crutzen acknowledged that the word Anthropocene had already been used in the 1980s by the Swedish ecologist Eugene F. Stoermer. This is why Crutzen and Stoermer coauthored the 2000 foundational article on the Anthropocene, published in the Global Change Newsletter Bulletin.

It was this article, precisely, that complicated the origin story of the Anthropocene. By inviting Stoermer, Crutzen not only acknowledged that someone else had used the term before his extemporary intervention in Cuernavaca, but also that the concept of the Anthropocene had a much longer history. In that article, Crutzen and Stoermer listed what would then become the canonical genealogy of the Anthropocene. The US diplomat and eclectic scholar George Perkins Marsh, with his 1864 book *Man and Nature*, is often recognized among the first to uncover the destructive and persistent character of human actions on the environment. Having read so many volumes published in Italian in the nineteenth century pointing to the systemic links connecting deforestation, floods, landslides, and climatic alterations, I have always wondered whether Marsh's primacy were mostly the result of the Anglophone imperialism.[3] Nonetheless, *Man and Nature* and its author are regularly listed among the precursors of the Anthropocene narrative. It could not be differently with such opening words:

> The object of the present volume is to indicate the character and, approximately, the extent of the changes produced by human action in the physical conditions of the globe we inhabit. (Marsh 1965 [1864], 3)

Although deeply rooted within the nature of the Mediterranean world – Marsh was a US diplomat in the Ottoman Empire and Italy – *Man and Nature* has an extraordinary global ambition, as exemplified from these telling opening words. The same global perspective on humans' effects on the environment was present in the writing of the Italian geologist Antonio Stoppani. In his 1873 geology handbook, Stoppani had indicated the emergence of the Anthropozoic, a new geological era marked by the "telluric" power of humans' activities. In the first decades of the twentieth century, the French philosopher and Jesuit priest Pierre Teilhard de Chardin and the Russian scientist Vladimir Vernadsky developed the concept of the noosphere – marking the beginning of a new age dominated by scientific knowledge and technology. In his compendium of the Anthropocene's genealogies, environmental historian Gregg Mitman has also included the US geologist Thomas Chamberlin, proponent in 1883 of the Psychozoic era, which assumed that humans were leaving their traces in the stratigraphy of the earth (2019, 61–64). Yet it is Mitman again who reminds us that this long genealogy of the Anthropocene has also been criticized by scholars who wish to underline the rupture of the Anthropocene rather than its continuity with past concepts and interpretations. According to Clive Hamilton, an Australian scholar who has been extremely active in the climate change debate, the radical novelty of the Anthropocene relies on the premise that there is something called the Earth System, that is, the interconnected assemblage of physical, chemical, and biological processes of which life is an integral part. For Hamilton, the mistake is to think of the Anthropocene within the usual individual disciplines, which seem to interpret it as just another word for the human modification of ecosystems. Instead, looking at it through Earth System Sciences implies recognizing the Anthropocene as a rupture in planetary cycles (Hamilton 2017, 17).

While Hamilton's critique of some Anthropocene narratives aims to reinforce the novelty – therefore the power – of the concept per se, the emergence of this new concept has spurred quite a heated debate among social scientists,

---

[3] For instance Afan de Rivera 1825; Gautieri 1815; Melograni 1810. On this Vecchio 1974.

humanities scholars, and artists. Perhaps, it is worth mentioning that the Anthropocene has acquired intellectual currency independently from the actual official deliberation of the International Commission on Stratigraphy. The main critique against the Anthropocene regards the alleged neutrality of the concept, its depoliticizing effect, its blindness toward social, historical, gender, and racial differences. The Anthropocene is the "age of humans", that is, an age in which "we" have affected the bio-geo-chemical cycles of the earth. Cohorts of progressive scholars have almost immediately signaled their discomfort with this universalistic narrative. For them – I should probably say for us – the "we" of the Anthropocene risks depicting humans as an undifferentiated community. On April 15, 2019, climate activists around the world used the image of the Notre Dame on fire to convey their message: our common home is on fire and "we" all must work together to save it. This metaphor perfectly exemplifies the controversial use of the word "we", or, at least, of the limitations of the Anthropocene universalism. Playing with that metaphor, one might argue that, when on fire, the house becomes "ours" and everybody is called on duty to extinguish the flames, but when there is no fire, those who own, or believe to own, the house, are much less inclined to welcome everybody into it. Nice homes with pools and drinkable water generally come with fences and security; not a *common home* in that case. Environmental humanities scholar Rob Nixon has nicely articulated this tension between universalism and injustice, writing that "[w]e may all be in the Anthropocene but we're not all in it in the same way" (Nixon 2019, 8). Similarly, I have used the Titanic disaster as a storytelling tool to discuss the tensions between the collective "we" of the Anthropocene – given that, indeed, humans are all together on the same boat, the earth – and the extreme unequal effects of the shipwreck on different groups of people (Armiero 2019). When on April 14, 1912, an iceberg collided with the Titanic, whether you traveled first or third class determined whether you lived or died. Quite literally, the Titanic metaphor says this loud and clear: class matters in the Anthropocene. Probably all my readers already know Chakrabarty's four theses and his argument for a species' history (2009) quite well. For all the richness of that debate, although recognizing the immense chasm between humans and nonhuman beings in the unfolding of the ecological crisis, I maintain my critique of the universalistic "we" of the Anthropocene.

I do not aim to build my handy strawman argument by blaming all earth system scientists for being blind toward social, environmental, and historical inequalities. Ian Angus has already shown that many of them are indeed aware of the social inequalities embedded into the Anthropocene (Angus 2016, 224–232). Will Steffen, one of the most influential earth system scientists, has often referred to the need to subvert structural power inequalities in order to create a sustainable future. He also agreed to work together with Indian sociologist Amita Baviskar and myself at the 2015 Anthropocene Campus in Berlin on a teaching module which was anything but a neutral and apolitical interpretation of the concept. Neither do I believe that all humanities and social science scholars who employ the word Anthropocene are ignorant of the power relations which organize our positionality in the new epoch. Nonetheless, I believe that the ways in which we speak of the Anthropocene do reflect our focus or perhaps priorities; and what I want to prioritize, or place at center stage, are the unjust socio-ecological relationships which make the universal "we" of the Anthropocene narrative an extremely abstract concept. To be blunt here: I do not think that it will be a label that will change unjust relationships, but whatever words we will use, we need to change the narrative they convey. If we agree that the human species as a whole is not responsible for the Anthropocene, we can also thereby reevaluate its origins and more importantly, I would argue, the possible exit strategies. Among those who support the species narrative, the Neolithic revolution (circa 12,000 years ago), with its invention/discovery of agriculture and animal domestication, is often considered the logical candidate for the starting point of the Anthropocene. This hypothesis, however, contradicts the idea of the Anthropocene as a major rupture in the earth's history; therefore, the Industrial Revolution in the eighteenth century and the so-called Great Acceleration of the post WWII years are generally considered the most appropriate turning points for the beginning of the new epoch. Crutzen and Stoermer themselves indicated the Industrial Revolution, with the connected explosion of CO_2 emissions, as the obvious candidate for the origin of the Anthropocene. Others, instead, have pointed to the extraordinary growth of the post-WWII years, with the exponential increase of almost everything connected to human activities, from urbanization to fishing, including the numbers of McDonald's restaurants around the world. This Great Acceleration (McNeill & Engelke 2016) has been immortalized in the iconic hockey stick graphics which show how from the 1950s onwards, almost all human related activities have skyrocketed. Furthermore, the Great Acceleration also provides an indelible marker in the geosphere: the radionuclide fallout of the atomic explosions occurring from 1945 onwards.

As I hope is clear to the reader, establishing the starting point of the Anthropocene is neither just a curiosity exercise nor a specialistic puzzle for geologists. As with everything in the Anthropocene – and with the environmental crisis – even this origin issue is highly controversial and inherently political. I have no hesitation in saying that this debate goes beyond the factual discoveries of the Geological Working Group. In this Element, as in general in the environmental humanities debates, the Anthropocene is analyzed as a global narrative about the current ecological crisis, rather than as a geological conundrum to be solved by scientists. Precisely for this reason, I find the debate generated by Lewis and Maslin on their "Orbis spike" hypothesis extremely productive. In brief, Lewis and Maslin propose the European invasion of the Americas as the starting point for the Anthropocene. They argue that the colonization of the New World not only had the characteristics of a planetary change in the earth's biota, but it also left a clear mark in the geosphere in the form of a significant decline in atmospheric CO_2 (circa 7–10 p.p.m.), as recorded in two Antarctic ice cores (Lewis & Maslin 2018). According to Lewis and Maslin, the causes of this remarkable decrease in atmospheric CO_2 lie in the combined mass-destruction of Indigenous people and the following reduction of agricultural practices and (re)expansion of forests.[4] While the proponents of the "Orbis hypothesis" give great importance to the materiality of their "golden spike" embedded within the ice core of Antarctica, instead, I would like to stress another point in their narrative, which I believe is more relevant in my critical exploration of the Anthropocene. The origin (hi)stories of the Anthropocene say something about who and what we consider responsible for the ecological crisis. "The Orbis spike," Lewis and Maslin write, "implies that colonialism, global trade and coal brought about the Anthropocene. Broadly, this highlights social concerns, particularly the unequal power relationships between different groups of people, economic growth, the impacts of globalized trade, and our current reliance on fossil fuels" (Lewis & Maslin 2018, 177). In this sense, I would say that the colonial origins of the Anthropocene are crystallized not only in two ice cores from Antarctica but in an equally visible manner within the racist arrangement of our societies and of the stories we tell about ourselves. As Laura Pulido (2019) has clearly stated, concealing racism in the (hi)story of the Anthropocene is a powerful way to divide colonialism from capitalism, as if they were independent from one another. Instead, following Cedric Robinson, Laura Pulido reminds us that racism is not an accident in capitalism but its very foundation. Introducing Cedric Robinson's classic *Black Marxism*, Robin Kelley wrote that "Capitalism and racism ... did not break from the old order but rather evolved from it to produce a modern world system of 'racial capitalism' dependent on slavery, violence, imperialism, and genocide" (Kelley 1983, xiii). The "Whitemanocene" would find its starting point at the intersection of colonialism, slavery, and capitalism. According to Janae Davis and her coauthors, the

---

[4] Clive Hamilton has challenged the "Orbis hypothesis" arguing that Lewis and Maslin could prove neither the human origin of the decreasing in CO_2 nor the fact that it changed the Earth System. Furthermore, according to Hamilton, a change of ten parts per million should be considered within the limits of normal variability in the atmosphere (Hamilton 2017, 23).

concept of the "Plantationocene" has the potential to bridge in one narrative the violence of racial capitalism and the "liberatory potential of Black ecologies" (Davis et al. 2018, 4). Indeed, (racial) capitalism is a central concept in any critical appraisal of the Anthropocene; placing it in that history implies a critique of species universalism by default, as well as a less flattening narrative about its causes. It is for this reason that the most successful alternative to the Anthropocene label has become the Capitalocene, the Age of Capitalism.[5] Jason Moore – the most vocal advocate of this concept – has defined the Capitalocene as the era of "capitalism as a world-ecology of power, capital, and nature" (Moore 2016, 6). Hence, capitalism does not stand here merely for an economic and social system, rather it "signifies capitalism as a way of organizing nature as a multispecies, situated, capitalist world-ecology" (Moore 2016, 6). Capitalocene embodies the crucial critiques against the Anthropocene narrative, while building an alternative storytelling that begs for the politicization of the current socio-ecological crisis. Speaking of the Capitalocene has liberated creativity among humanities and social sciences scholars, igniting a proliferation of possible alternatives to the label "Anthropocene," including the Plantationocene (Haraway 2015; Tsing 2015), Econocene (Norgaard 2013), Technocene (Hornborg 2015), Anthrobscene (Parikka 2015; Ernstson & Swyngedouw 2019), and Manthropocene (Raworth 2014; Di Chiro 2017). In the end, these diverse labels all aim to counter what has been perceived as the blind spot of the Anthropocene narrative, that is, its invisibilization, or at least undervaluation, of social, historical, racial, and gender inequalities in the paths toward the contemporary ecological crisis.

2.2 The Case for the Wasteocene

The Wasteocene is only one of the (too) many alternative "-cenes" that especially radical scholars have been putting forward, stimulating a more critical debate about the Anthropocene and its (hi)stories. It can be said that at the very core of every Anthropocene story lies some kind of waste. Apparently, the Age of Humans is marked by a techno-stratigraphy of wasted matter, such as carbon sediments, radionuclides and microplastics, accumulating beneath the earth's surface. Waste can be considered the essence of the Anthropocene, embodying humans' ability to affect the environment to the point of transforming it into a gigantic dump. For this reason, Massimo De Angelis and I have proposed to

---

[5] In his volume *Anthropocene or Capitalocene?*, Jason Moore offers a brief account of the genesis of the word Capitalocene, acknowledging Andreas Malm's initial intuition but also suggesting a rhizomatic and independent use of the word by several scholars, including David Ruccio, Donna Haraway, and himself with Tony Weis (Moore 2016, 5).

call the new epoch the Wasteocene (Armiero & De Angelis 2017). As much as the materiality of waste accumulating everywhere in our environment can provide a plain explanation for our concept, Wasteocene is not about waste as an object. Rather, thinking of the Wasteocene means to frame waste as wasting, that is, as socio-ecological relations creating wasted people and wasted places. The Wasteocene, then, is not the age where waste is everywhere; it is not a fancy academic label for lamenting the dirtiness of our cities. Neither is it another word for the familiar environmentalist nostalgia for some paradise, lost in the past. Actually, the Wasteocene is about cleanliness and aseptic environments as much as it is about griminess and contamination. Because at its very essence, wasting implies sorting out what has value and what does not. Zsuzsa Gille has written of the inherent classification and displacement connected to any waste regime, that is, to the social organization determining what is waste and where it should go (2007, 21; 34). The dump is a function of the safe and green neighborhood. As the US writer Rebecca Solnit (2008) has brilliantly argued, it is the wall that makes the paradise, that is, the othering of someone or something that creates a safe "us." Wasting is a social process through which class, race, and gender injustices become embedded into the socio-ecological metabolism producing both gardens and dumps, healthy and sick bodies, pure and contaminated places. I believe that the Wasteocene can be understood only within the wider concept of Capitalocene; it is one of the manifold manifest-ations of capitalist ecologies producing the contemporary crisis. However, through the Wasteocene, I intend to stress the contaminated nature of capitalism and its endurance within the texture of life. While the traces of the Anthropocene are looked upon into the geosphere, the Wasteocene requires an exploration of what we might call the organosphere, that is, the texture of life. Strata of toxicity have been laid within bodies of human and nonhuman beings, testifying for the oppression and exploitation that capitalism has imposed upon subalterns.[6] The Wasteocene is inherently historical because it implies the persistence of waste; it is synchronized with what Rob Nixon (2011) has labeled "slow violence," that is, the delayed effects of environmental harms on humans, nonhumans, and ecosystems. As the Capitalocene speaks of the origins, or better, the causes, of the socio-ecological crisis, the Wasteocene uncovers the effects of capitalism on life. The Anthropocene is not only blind, or at least reticent, toward the responsibilities of the crisis, it also leaves open the possi-bility to interpret the new era in radically diverse ways. Some have been speaking of a "good Anthropocene," arguing that the age of humans can be an

---

[6] Similarly, Massimo De Angelis has written about detritus as "the layers of waste inscribed in the body and in the environment" due to the capitalist organization of life (2007, 70–71).

opportunity for finally taking total control of the planet.[7] If this is the age of humans, let the humans rule the planet without any further quandary – this is the basic message of the good Anthropocene's prophets. From this point of view, speaking of the Wasteocene does not leave any doubt about the inherent nature of the new epoch. We may all agree that it is not going to be easy to propose a good Wasteocene.

As the Wasteocene is not about the material stuff but the socio-ecological relationships making someone/something disposable, as a concept it also questions some basic corollaries of the mainstream Anthropocene narrative. First of all, placing socio-ecological relations at its core, Wasteocene unmasks and rejects any form of reification, which seems quite a relevant feature in the Anthropocene discourse. It implies, for instance, that it is not CO_2 emissions that have created the ecological crisis, but socio-ecological relationships that produce the emissions. CO_2 emissions, as any other kind of waste, are often seen as technical problems demanding technical solutions. An expert or a scientist will save us. In times of post-truth narratives, when science is questioned on narrow partisan grounds and an anti-intellectual wave accompanies the rise of populist and xenophobic movements, my critique of scientific expertise as the solution to the socio-ecological crisis can easily be misunderstood. Science has indeed not only indicated the problems humanity is facing, but also contributed to finding solutions. My argument here is that we cannot and should not bypass the complicated and always conflictual space of politics. Because, if the problem is the "thing" – be it the CO_2 emissions or any kind of waste – geo-engineering, atomic energy, or incinerators *can* be the solutions; but if we wish to tackle the socio-ecological relationships that feed a few with profits and power to the detriment of the many, we may need to change these relationships. Wasteocene also features and uncovers another characteristic of the Anthropocene discourse: with waste it is extremely common to blame those who are more affected for having created the problem in the first place. Precisely as shown by the Anthropocene discourse. But the Wasteocene repoliticizes the socio-ecological crisis; wasting is a relationship – not a thing or a mistake to be solved. As a storytelling dispositif, Wasteocene has the power to speak the truth, taking injustices not as almost invisible side effects but as the centerpiece of a system that produces wealth and security through the othering of those who must be excluded.

An important corollary of the shift from the Anthropocene to the Wasteocene lies in the centrality of the body, which is a space of both oppression and liberation. While the Anthropocene may seem a distant concept, almost literally

---

[7] On the good Anthropocene see Hamilton 2015.

buried under layers of rocks or trapped in the deep sky, the Wasteocene is immanent, always so close that one can feel or smell it. The body – both human and nonhuman – is at the very center of the Wasteocene. In the pages of this Element, I will argue that the body has often functioned as a detector of the Wasteocene. It has been biological – rather than geologic – excavations into the living tissues of the planet which have shown us that a new epoch has begun. The body is a powerful tool, a porous space, as Stacy Alaimo (2010) has taught us, which absorbs and makes visible the toxic soup sponging everything on earth. The Wasteocene is internal, it is embodied, it is made of flesh, blood, and dirt. As the Anthropocene meshes with the planetary boundaries drawn by Ian Rockström and his team (2009), the Wasteocene should bring the bodily boundaries which design the safe operating space for the survival of life right to the forefront. Capitalism continuously pumps toxins into the life system of the planet, following its own boundary logic. Those are the boundaries severing privilege and disposability, purity and contamination, life and death. One might say that capitalism's conatus will, sooner or later, lead to the disruption of those boundaries and the wasting of everything. Indeed, we are all on the same boat, or planet; but, as on the Titanic, rest assured that armed guards and locked gates will do their best to patrol the borders between those who are destined to drown and those who need to be saved. Actually, I would argue that the more we enter into the Wasteocene, the stronger this securitization and exclusion becomes. The livable space within the bodily boundaries of the Wasteocene is narrowing, therefore requiring higher fences and stricter access controls. What is the Mediterranean Sea nowadays if not the epitome of the Wasteocene, the conceptual and material border against which thousands of humans crash in their attempt to force the boundaries dividing those who value and those who are disposable?

But the centrality of the body in the Wasteocene does not speak only of oppression and victimization. The bodily experience of the Wasteocene has also produced resisting subjects. As wasting is a social relation reproducing power inequalities, it is inherently a political and not a technical fact. Entering the bodies and the ecologies of humans and nonhumans, wasting politicizes bodies and ecologies. The disposable body becomes a political body and its struggle to survive an insurrection or, more mimetically, a sabotage of the social relationships which enforce the bodily boundaries of the Wasteocene. As I will argue in section 5, the nemesis of wasting is not recycling but commoning. With this, I do not mean to disvalue recycling or any other practice of waste reduction based on individual choices and engagement. On the contrary, I believe that recycling may contain some pillars of commoning, including an attitude to think of reproduction (vs. consumption). Actually, I agree with Finn-Arne Jørgensen that recycling can have a broader positive effect by leading us "to rethink our relationship with matter around us" (2019, x). Nonetheless, as my focus is on wasting rather than waste, I maintain that commoning is the antidote. By "commoning" I mean the ensemble of socio-ecological practices which (re) produce commons, transforming it from a "thing" into a collective practice, a relationship. With Negri and Hardt, we can say that commons are both what we share and the social infrastructure for sharing it (2017, 97). As commons and commoning have the property of self-regeneration through a network of socio-ecological relationships (De Angelis 2017, 227–9), I argue that commoning is to (re)production through sharing as wasting is to extraction through othering. In other words, while wasting relationships are based on consuming and "other-ing," that is, on sorting out what and who is waste, commoning practices are based on reproducing resources and communities.

2.3 Wasting Futures

The Wasteocene has not received much attention from scientists; nonetheless, it has indeed become an important trope in the narratives about our collective futures. I would argue that more than scientists, writers and filmmakers have remarkably influenced our collective imaginaries about the future, and waste, in its manifold forms, has often been a key feature of those imagined futures. As the apocalypse has become the norm through which the future is imagined, waste is often its aesthetic manifestation. Writing about apocalypse in science fiction literature, Heather Hicks has spoken of the "globalized ruin" as the cipher of that narrative (2016, 7). Anna Tsing has been especially influential in exploring the epistemological potentialities of ruins and ruined landscapes. In her volume *The Mushroom at the End of the World*, Tsing argues that "[t]o know the world that progress has left to us, we must track shifting patches of ruination" (2015, 206). More generally, Tsing hints at a correlation between fantasies of modernization and ruination (208); and indeed, ruins are the ultimate manifestation of extreme modernity. While most science fiction speculations envision ruins as the product of some abrupt apocalypse, whatever it may be, Tsing stresses the normality of ruination, the almost mundane production of a world of ruins, as if the shift from what we perceive as livable vis-à-vis what is waste would occur imperceptibly, more like a continuum than a fracture. In the introduction to *Arts of Living on a Damaged Planet*, Tsing, Gan, Swanson, and Bubandt, express this concept with great clarity:

> As humans reshape the landscape, we forget what was there before. Ecologists call this forgetting the "shifting baseline syndrome." Our newly shaped and ruined landscapes become the new reality. (2017, 6)

This friction between an abrupt shift and a slow transition is quite significant. Of course, generously employing the trope of the apocalypse, science fiction leans more toward the traumatic fracture breaking (into) modernity. For the sake of my argument, sudden shift or slow transition are not extremely relevant. Rather, what is relevant is the idea of ruination as a fracture which breaks modernity, often it is even the byproduct of modernity. The post-apocalypse world is always a world of ruins. This means that in science fiction narratives, the future is deeply haunted by the past, literally built from its ruins. The Wasteocene in science fiction has the face of ruins, of the remains of a modernity which is now unable to function; it is modernity turned into waste. As the world is transformed into a gigantic dump, humans are often depicted as scavengers in a perpetual quest for salvaging something from the scraps of the past. Scavenging for food is, as it should logically be, almost an obsession in post-apocalyptic movies. In *The Road*, for instance, the cinematic transposition of Cormac McCarthy's 2006 novel, the two unnamed protagonists – a father and his son – are always looking for food while moving in a completely wasted landscape toward an imaginary community in the US West. The quest for food is even more significant in the plot since most of the survivors have turned to cannibalism in order to feed themselves. The ruin of modernity does not only reflect onto the dilapidated landscape around the protagonists; it enters their bodies, radically changing the very nature of their being humans. The dehumanization of the post-apocalyptic world is a staple in the science fiction narrative. The entire *Mad Max* saga, perhaps one of the most effective cinematic representations of the post-apocalypse world, blends the material ruins of a world in pieces with the almost spiritual ruins of survivors who have lost their humanity. In *Mad Max,* as in many other science fiction narratives, the scraps of modernity are reused and re-signified in a bricolage which seems to be the essence of the imagined Wasteocene.

In this sense, science fiction narratives confirm what Serenella Iovino once wrote, that "[waste] symbolizes the inherent corruption upon which every society is built" (2009, 340). Indeed, those survivors inhabit a world in ruins but they seem able to make sense of those messy remnants of a past comfort, moving through waste as if it were their natural environment. Yet I believe that science fiction narratives become even more powerful when they deliver the main message of the Wasteocene, that is, the othering project which simultaneously produces the global dump for the most and the paradise for the few. The very contrast between a world of debris and one of perfection is the plastic image of the Wasteocene, which, as I argue all along this Element, implies cleanliness and purity just as much as waste and toxicity. Because what really matters is the demarcation between the two worlds or, in other words, the socio-ecological relationships creating both.

The Brazilian television series *3%* is a wonderful science fiction transposition of the Wasteocene logic. In a not too distant future, the Brazilian society is divided between a poor and dilapidated "inland" and the utopic and almost paradisiac "offshore." Technology is the most crucial gap dividing the two worlds: while the offshore is packed with all sorts of futuristic gadgets, the inland looks like a gigantic favela where people survive out of scraps. *3%* represents the contrast between clean and modern vs dirty and obsolete. While science is the offshore's guiding principle, bricolage seems to be the most relevant knowledge for the inland; being able to reuse/repurpose what was wasted is a crucial skill for those who are forced to live in a social and material dump. So far, *3%* is not dramatically different from other post-apocalyptic stories, perhaps only more explicit in its representation of wasting socio-ecological relationships. *3%* becomes more unique and interesting when it explains the procedures for the selection of those who can move to the offshore. Using science fiction to convey the neoliberal credo of competition and meritocracy, the authors imagine that every year all the newly turned 18-year-old citizens can participate in a complex and manipulative series of tests – "O Processo," The Process – through which some of them will be selected and transferred to the offshore. From the Wasteocene point of view, "O Processo" is a key dispositif because it illustrates creatively – nonetheless quite realistically – the interiorization of the wasting relationships reproducing wasted people and places. In this science fiction dystopia, there is even some kind of religion worshipping "O Processo" – thus rendering all the dispossessed people from the inland completely governamentalized and obedient to the unjust logic separating those who deserve more from those who are not considered. At the beginning of the third season, Michele, one of the leaders of the rebellion against the system, clearly states that for the rich people living in the offshore, the rest of the population was simply waste. Violent repression is a crucial means in the *3%* as well as in the real Wasteocene; people do not easily accept to be treated as waste and forced to live in socio-ecological dumps. Nonetheless, the epistemic and cultural repression is also an important tool for keeping the system working. In this sense, the idea of O Processo is extremely powerful because it refers to the paraphernalia of neoliberal lies about deserving "a better life" through one's own merits and hard work. Similarly to what Bauman has argued (2007, 136), this discourse of merits supposes that those who live in the global socio-ecological dump are not victims of injustice but rather of their own inability to build a better life for themselves. The Wasteocene is not about the ruins of the inland – to employ the *3%* narrative – it is instead about how much they are the by-product of unjust socio-ecological relationships normalized through an almost religious celebration. At a certain point in the show, it becomes clear that the wasting of the inland was the direct effect of the flourishing of the offshore. Indeed, every paradise needs so badly a hell that it creates its own.

Very similar the idea behind *3%* is that behind the movie *Elysium*.[8] The plot almost seems the same: the earth is turned into a planetary slum, inhabited by poor people living among ruins and waste, while the elites have happily moved to a space station – unequivocally named *Elysium* – equipped with a bounty of futuristic technologies including an almost magic healing machine. In the *Elysium* narrative, more than that of *3%*, the ruination not only involves the landscape, but the very bodies of the people living on earth. With an impressive resemblance to reality, *Elysium* offers a science fiction transposition of the Wasteocene that revolves around two main tropes: the sick' body and the migrant. The people living on the ground do not just move among a ruined landscape, they embody that ruination within their own bodies. Everyone seems to be somehow broken, sick, wasted in their own physical humanity. Their bodies, as well as the land they inhabit, are dumps, wasted matters of no value other than being disposable. All these themes are exemplified in the story of the white male hero: working in an extremely harmful factory, he becomes terminally ill because his boss forces him to do a task which exposes him to a lethal dose of radiations. Once sick, he is nothing more than a disposable object, thus he decides to bricolage his body with the scraps of more advanced technologies, transforming himself into a handmade cyborg on the quest for justice. His mission becomes smuggling a young sick girl onto the *Elysium* space station so she can access the superior healing technologies available to the rich. The interconnection of ill bodies, inequalities, and exclusion are at the very core of the Wasteocene: the production of wasted people and places goes hand in hand with the construction of global gated communities. The attempt to force open the doors of *Elysium* and access its privileges is a perfect metaphor for the present migration crisis; after all, Fortress Europe, Australia, and the United States are in their essence Wasteocene in the making. Sealing off their frontiers, the rich countries state loud and clear that there is a border between who is worth it and who is disposable. Keeping the order of things and establishing who must stand on each side of that border is what the Wasteocene is all about.

3 Wasteocene Stories

3.1 Domesticating Memories, Toxic Narratives, Wasted Stories

As a historian, I have always struggled with my weak memory, and, for sure, things are not improving with age. I remember my anxiety when, as a professor,

---

[8] On this see Giuliani 2021.

some students would start listing a rosary of dates of battles or treaties of which I was not sure at all. Indeed, historians are supposed to remember; someone might say that preserving the collective memory of the past is the core business of our discipline. Perhaps dates, battles, and treaties have gone out of fashion in the last few decades; more radically, the postmodernist turn may have gone so far as to challenge the very autonomy of the past vis-à-vis the ways in which we tell stories about it. Without indulging in any radical relativism, I do believe that the main role of historians is not simply remembering the past, but rather organizing the collective memory, something which implies forgetting as much as remembering. By shaping the official knowledge of the past, professional historians draw the map of what should belong to our memory, and thereby, to our identities. And, as in every respectable map, what is omitted is as important as what stays in.

History textbooks are the ultimate instruction booklets for the use of the past; and, clearly, what is expunged from the organized memory and its official reproduction can be as instructive as what is deemed worth preserving and what will therefore be passed through generations. Reflecting on the representation of Japanese imperialism in Asia, Peter Cave has written that "[history textbooks'] unique role in educating children about the past, especially the national past, makes them a crucial battleground upon which diverging views about national identity can be fought out" (2013, 542–3). The importance of controlling the transmission of collective memory has always been clear to the people in power, especially those who struggle the most with accepting the value of democratic pluralism. In Bolsonaro's Brazil, the minister of Education Ricardo Vélez campaigned to change the history textbooks in order to give a more "balanced vision" – that is, more positive – on the 1964 military coup which removed the left-wing government in power (BBC 2019). In 2011, Berlusconi's party proposed a parliamentary inquiry into the Italian history textbooks, which were accused of having strong leftist bias, especially addressing the Resistance against Nazi-Fascist regime (Luppino 2011). According to a *New York Times* reportage, in the United States the same history textbooks have been adjusted to the diverse political climates of the states; Texas and California, for instance, do not seem to share the same national history (Goldstein 2020). The president of the Association of Hungarian History Teachers stated that the aim of the government interventions in education was "to create a version of history preferable to Orbán" (Kingsley 2018). The president Vladimir Putin also engaged with the (re)production of historical narratives campaigning for a more unifying representation of Russian history, a demand which led Russia's Historical Society to produce 80-page long guidelines for the writing of history handbooks (Baczynska 2013). The examples could multiply indefinitely, but the main message would be the same: "Knowledge is a form of power," as Howard Zinn puts it.

In modern times – Zinn continues – when social control rests on "the consent of the governed," force is kept in abeyance for emergencies, and everyday control is exercised by a set of rules, a fabric of values passed on from one generation to another by the priests and teachers of the society. What we call the rise of democracy in the world means that force is replaced by deception (a blunt way of saying "education") as the chief method for keeping society as it is. (1970, 6)

The way in which we tell stories about our past is paramount to the construction of collective –mostly national – identities and it gives a sense of direction to the present and the future. Historians have often acted as the guardians at the gates of the past or, less poetically, as traffic wardens trying to guide the flows of memories entering through those gates. Thinking through the lens of the Wasteocene, I argue that historians have also contributed to the making of the narrative infrastructure which ensures the reproduction of wasting relationships. Some stories, memories, or even facts must be wasted; they are not considered worth remembering. The other side of this systematic sorting of wasted stories has been the production of an Anthropocene "master's narrative," as Stefania Barca has called it in another Element of this series (Barca 2020) – that is, one which hides the systemic intersection of racism/colonialism, heteropatriarchy, class inequality and human supremacy in producing the planetary crisis. In identifying Humanity with the master of Nature, she claims, this hegemonic narrative hides the other-than-master subjects, discounting them as irrelevant to the story. A master's narrative, then, is not simply about what memories and subjectivities are wasted out of history telling, but even more, about how that master's narrative functions to justify that very exclusion. Wasteocene histories reproduce the wasting relationships that make some places and people disposable. To be fair, since the sixties and seventies social historians have worked to change the mainstream historical narrative, recovering bits and pieces from the memory's dump. Subaltern groups have entered the historical discourses through research on workers, women, slaves, Indigenous people, the poor, peasants, and many more marginal subjects – or objects. The convergence between the New Left and the students' movement in the Sixties and Seventies explains this democratization of history and the widening of "acceptable" subjects. The rise of environmental history has enlarged the scope of history even more, introducing themes which were previously unheard of; it became acceptable to write about rats in New York, forests in Brazil, or salmon in the American Northwest.[9] This shift was not easy and the struggle is nowhere near complete. When in 1999, I submitted my first book manuscript on the history of forests in an Italian region, an extremely influential historian

---

[9] Only as examples, see Biehler 2013, Dean 1995, and Taylor 1999.

commented sarcastically that at that rate scholars would have started writing about the most insignificant things. In the end, the manuscript was indeed published, but I would say that environmental history is, after twenty years, still quite weak, academically, in Italy, as well as in several other countries across the world. It is not so uncommon to still hear distinguished scholars protest about the lack of scientific reliability of oral history or lament the alleged dispersion of historical research across too wide and irrelevant topics.

Even acknowledging the widening of history and the proliferation of research on themes and subjects which were considered marginal in mainstream historical narratives, I still maintain that the (re)production of the collective memory – in other words, the construction of an official history and its transmission through education and public discourses – remains largely immune to these new lines of research. Erasing what does not fit in the mainstream narrative is the first and more common dispositif for producing Wasteocene histories. Commenting on the indifference of the Anthropocene master's narrative toward the astonishing number of earth defenders who are murdered each year, Stefania Barca writes:

> Narratives do not kill by themselves, of course. But they might hide the killings and the killed from view, and convince us that they are not part of the story of modernity. (Barca 2020).

Invisibilize violence, normalize injustice, erase any alternative narrative – these are the pillars of the Wasteocene narratives. Let me offer one example of these Wasteocene narratives from my research on the Italian mountains (Armiero 2011).

On October 9, 1963, 300 million cubic meters of rock crashed into the Vajont reservoir, provoking a gigantic wave which overcame the dam and destroyed the town of Longarone, killing 2000 people. The Vajont disaster is among the most tragic events in post-WWII Italian history, nonetheless, it was removed from the national collective memory. Apart from the works of a few historians, there are no traces of it in the official narrative of the so-called Italian economic miracle of the sixties.[10] It was thanks to the work of a theater actor and author, Marco Paolini, that in the late 1990s the history of Vajont entered the collective memory of the country with a two-hour-long monologue broadcasted by the public television. Evidently, the history of how modernity and economic growth had materialized in a remote valley through the arrogance of a powerful hydroelectric corporation and the complicity of the state did not fit well with the general narrative about Italy finally becoming a rich and modern society. The

---

[10] With "economic miracle" historians indicate the extraordinary economic growth occurring in Italy between the 1950s and 60s.

history of the Vajont disaster is a handbook example of the Wasteocene logic. In the name of progress and a superior "common good" (Roy 1999), some lives and some places were sacrificed, literally put at work for the wellbeing of others. The wasting relationships transforming a remote valley in a hydropower machine not only produced wasted lives – the immense cemetery of Longarone – but also wasted knowledges and memories. Indeed, wasted knowledges because locals did try to alert the authorities about the risks they foresaw coming from the dam, but they were either ignored or ridiculed. It was a battle between scientific knowledge and professional experts on one side and lay people from an Alpine valley on the other. The game was lost from the start. Wasting the memory of the Vajont implied erasing the disaster from the mainstream historical narrative, but also domesticating it. While invisibilization erases even the traces of what/who has been wasted, the domestication of memory is perhaps a more sophisticated strategy to continue reproducing wasting relationships. In cases as that of the Vajont, the domestication of memory means to arrange a certain version of history which neither unveils injustices nor gives room to social rage. Mourning the loss of human lives may be acceptable but it should be purified of any social implications. Thereby, the Vajont disaster was represented as just an unfortunate accident and its memory should bring peace and cohesion, not outrange and conflict. Recollecting her experience, Carolina, a survivor of the 1963 Vajont disaster, explained this process of domestication of memory:

> Institutions have done and do everything is in their power to divide the good survivors from the bad ones. The good ones are those who tell the story of suffering, those who move the listeners to tears, but then stop there. Those are the ones who shut up and leave to the institutions the task of telling the facts and therefore make memory harmless; in this way, memory does not disturb powerful economic interests which still prioritize profit over human lives. (Vastano 2014)

The Italian journalist Lucia Vastano (2008) has told the story of the cemetery of the Vajont victims in a way which I believe wonderfully proves my idea of the domestication of memory as wasting relationships by other means. In 2003, the municipal government of Longarone decided to transform the old cemetery of Fortogna, where the victims of the disaster were buried, into an official memorial. The old cemetery was razed to the ground, wasting once more the memories and symbols gathered there by the survivors, including this tombstone of the Paiola family (seven deaths, including three children):

> Brutally and cowardly murdered by the inattention and human greed, still waiting in vain for justice for this infamous fault. Premeditated massacre. (Vastano 2008, 157)

In the new cemetery, the memory of the victims was geometrically organized through marble blocks bearing only the names of the deceased; the mourning has to be domesticated, the Wasteocene logic cannot be questioned. If a tragic episode makes the waste of human lives too evident to be hidden, this must be understood as an accident and not as the epiphany of the Wasteocene, the proof that the system is grounded in the wasting of humans and nonhumans, their lives, their knowledge, even their stories.

In the Vajont story, the domestication of memories, so plastically built into the tale of the two cemeteries, goes hand in hand with the fabrication of toxic narratives, another mark of the Wasteocene. The collective of Italian radical writers Wu Ming (2013) has defined a toxic narrative

> A story which is always told from the same point of view, in the same way, even with the same words, omitting always the same details and removing the same elements which might offer a sense of the context and its complexity.

Toxic narratives are close relatives of what Latinx scholars have called "majoritarian stories" (Solórzano & Yosso 2002), that is, stories which naturalize racial privilege while either dismissing or erasing the experience of people who do not conform to the White paradigm. Linking narratives and toxicity is extremely appealing in the thinking of the Wasteocene because, as Serenella Iovino (2016, 168) has argued, pollution is always a concoction where harmful chemical substances blend with harmful discourses. Toxic narratives build the storytelling infrastructure which hinder the possibility to even see the injustice while blaming the affected communities for problems caused not by them, of course, but rather by the Wasteocene logic of othering people and places. The Vajont case offers both the domestication of memory, which I have illustrated above, and the engineering of toxic narratives. To brew the perfect toxic narrative, the first ingredient is concealing; the over-spilling of the Wasteocene logic – whether it is a dam disaster or the slow violence of industrial production – has to disappear from the collective memory. The second ingredient is naturalizing/normalizing injustice: if something bad occurs, it is nobody's fault. Sorrow, not outrage, is the right sentiment. Thirdly, it is vital to dismiss any kind of knowledge and experience, which may prove that other points of view existed; this is what always happens to those who try to denounce toxicity while resisting the wasting relationships that render them disposable. Finally, the ultimate result of a toxic narrative is to blame the victims; if one is on the wrong side of the Wasteocene line, it must be their fault. Waste is an ontological quality and not the product of unjust socio-ecological relationships – this is the main message of any toxic narrative. And it is against it that any counter-narrative must rise up.

3.2 Guerrilla Narrative in the Wasteocene Jungle

The fact that toxic narratives are so powerful and the domestication of memories does not allow any antagonist ways of remembering only implies that the stories of the Wasteocene are more difficult to be seen. Nonetheless, those stories are out there, resisting silencing and invisibilization. Before being razed to the ground, the old cemetery of the Vajont was one of those places where the counter-narratives of the Wasteocene became visible, and therefore, they had to be silenced/domesticated. Perhaps the cemetery is the extreme repository of those counter-narratives from the other side of the Wasteocene. Literally, those are voices from the underworld; there, wasted bodies perform a peculiar form of storytelling in which the memories of the survivors and the structural violence of the Wasteocene are embodied into an affective and material landscape. Indeed, a cemetery can be a telling archive of the Wasteocene, especially when it is marginal enough to be protected from the domestication of memories which occurred, for instance, in the Vajont case. Not always are the tombstones so telling as in the case of the Paiola family; more often, one needs a living guide who can connect the dead and the living. As Phaedra Pezzullo has written, a visit to the Holy Rosary Cemetery is a must in the Toxic Tour through the heavily contaminated region of Louisiana called Cancer Alley (2003, 241). In his research on Italian miners in Belgium, Daniele Valisena (2020, 288–293) also ends up in a cemetery, in Seraing. Walking through the graves, Valisena is able to 'listen to' the wasted stories of generations of workers whose bodies became gears in the treadmill of the capitalistic production of coal. The magnitude of the cemetery, the age of the deceased (generally in their fifties), the paraphernalia of objects and photographs from this old mining universe, and the shift in the nationalities of the people buried there (visible in the names carved on the tombstones) tell stories about the cycle of coal extraction, migrations, and human consumption in the mines. That cemetery – as well as many others around the world – is a silent storyteller of the Wasteocene. Its embodied materiality, made of bodies, words, images, and stones, tells the stories of wasted lives, people placed on the other side of the Wasteocene line, where humans and their memories can be disposed of. Reflecting on the appalling story of Taranto and its subjugation to a gigantic steel factory, the Italian intellectual Adriano Sofri wrote:

> The truth about Taranto should not be searched looking at the red fences of Ilva [the steel factory], at the two splendid and poisoned seas [in front of the town], or at the dark wall that defends an empty military arsenal from anyone. One should visit the cemetery of San Brunone above Tamburi [the working-class neighborhood close to the factory]. The remains of those who have to be

buried await in cold storage rooms, the poorest of the posthumous destin-
ations, because the earth is too polluted to be handled by workers . . .. Among
the thousand ways to investigate how much and how you die in Taranto, there
is also this, the patient reading of the birth and death dates on the tombstones.
(Sofri 2013)

Following Sofri's suggestion, the anonymous author of a short reportage from
San Brunone cemetery stressed how the people from Taranto have to bear the
factory even in the afterlife (Erodoto108, 2014). Roaming around the graves,
the author notices that the tombstones are completely covered in the red dust
from the factory, while a skyline made of chimneys and hills of coal closes the
horizon of life and death in Taranto. The author notices a tombstone from 1934
whose inscription said that the man buried there was killed by his job – indeed,
the Wasteocene logic which makes someone disposable is older than the steel
factory. Although in environmental justice literature, cemeteries are often
included as one of the communities' places endangered by corporations, they
should also be considered as material archives of counter-hegemonic stories.
Cemeteries are, of course, privileges that not all wasted people are allowed to
have. We should remember the Indigenous people killed without any right to be
buried or deprived of their ancestors' burial grounds, the women who disappeared without leaving any traces, the miners who were never recovered from
the bowels of the earth, the thousands migrants dead while crossing the
Mediterranean Sea. For the mass killing of nonhuman lives, we do not even
conceive the idea of a place for mourning.

Naomi Klein opens the documentary *Shock Doctrine* precisely by remarking
the importance of preserving communities' stories in order to resist the imposition of the capitalist disaster logic:

> It's what happens to us when we lose our narratives. When we lose our
> history, when we become disoriented. What keeps us oriented, and alert,
> and out of shock is our history.

If Naomi Klein is right and stories matter, the struggles in and against the
Wasteocene are also narrative struggles. I would dare to say that we should take
control of the means of production – and reproduction – of narratives because the
ways in which we narrate stories about the world affects the ways in which we
imagine and build a new one, or fall into the trap of rebuilding the same world all
over again. The imposition of toxic narratives and domesticated memories serves
the purpose of naturalizing and normalizing the Wasteocene; a guerrilla narrative,
then, serves to reveal the Wasteocene and dismantle its wasting logic.

I started to employ the expression "guerrilla narrative" in 2017, when together
with my former student Ilenia Iengo we began to expand our individual

collections of interviews on environmental injustice into a wider multimedia open-access archive. Thanks to a small grant, we were able to launch *ToxicBios. A Guerrilla Narrative Project* through which we gathered almost seventy "toxic autobiographies." To be honest, we did not have a clear understanding of what a "guerrilla narrative" could be; it was not a well-designed methodology, filled with the social science jargon which would have brought the appropriate respectable aura to the project. Speaking of guerrilla narrative was first and foremost a political gesture, a statement against the toxic narratives of the Wasteocene. Guerrilla narrative was not our scholarly invention, but a collage of subaltern practices of salvaging the stories and memories dumped by the Wasteocene regime. Those resisting stories have always been there in diverse forms; guerrilla narrative simply gives a name to those practices, making explicit their inherent antagonist character and the repression face of the mainstream narrative. The idea behind the guerrilla narrative is that toxic storytelling does not only uncover the traces of toxicity, exposing the injustice embedded into the Wasteocene, but it also frees an antagonist narrative which can potentially transform contaminated communities into resisting communities (see section 5 of this Element). Guerrilla narrative is quite close to what Critical Race Theorists, especially Latinx scholars, have written on majoritarian stories – what we call toxic narratives – and counter-stories. Solórzano and Yosso, for instance, define

> the counter-story as a method of telling the stories of those people whose experiences are not often told (i.e., those on the margins of society). The counter-story is also a tool for exposing, analyzing, and challenging the majoritarian stories of racial privilege. … Yet, counter-stories need not be created only as a direct response to majoritarian stories. … Indeed, within the histories and lives of people of color, there are numerous unheard counter-stories. Storytelling and counter-storytelling these experiences can help strengthen traditions of social, political, and cultural survival and resistance. (Solórzano & Yosso 2002, 32)

Indeed, as clearly expressed in the passage above, guerrilla narrative is both a rebellion against mainstream narrative and a quest for autonomy/alternatives; framing one's own storytelling only in opposition to the majoritarian story would reinforce the power of the latter and the subordination of the former.

Counter-hegemonic storytelling is always embodied insofar it is rooted into race and gender; however, in the ToxicBios project, that embodiment trespasses the border of the storyteller's body and becomes a more choral bodily narrative. The stories gathered in the ToxicBios digital platform are stories of the Wasteocene, they are intertwined with the texture of toxicity, which constitutes the invisible infrastructure which supports/reproduces wasting relationships through bodies, air, water, soil, species, and generations. Although humans are the storytellers in the ToxicBios project, they always frame their toxic stories in an intertwined network of life. Fish are integral part of Arlindo's biography, from his childhood memories to the present contamination (Marques 2017). Angela Rosa (2017) tells her story moving literally and discursively around the trees of her farm, which represent both the legacy of the past and the present of her struggle against GMOs. The story of the Cannavaccioulo family in Acerra, Italy, is a telling and tragic example of the interspecies connections which bind humans and nonhumans in the Wasteocene: theirs is a story of dioxin contamination which affected both their sheep – the Cannavaccioulos have been shepherds for generations – and their own bodies (Armiero & Fava 2016).

In the almost seventy stories included in the ToxicBios archive, the body is always a key element. As much as the Wasteocene aims to build impersonal, almost disembodied narratives, guerrilla narrative speaks from a specific, embodied, place-based standpoint. As the Wasteocene logic feeds itself through wasting people and places, the guerrilla narrative cannot escape from this wasted materiality in its quest for freedom and redemption. One must recognize to have been wasted, to live in the Wasteocene, in order to fight against it. The body can be a powerful sensor, a sort of window into the Wasteocene. In several of the stories collected through the ToxicBios project, the awareness of living on the wrong side of the Wasteocene divide rises through a sensorial experience. Bad smell – the stink – is probably the most recurrent trope in several of those toxic autobiographies (Armiero & De Rosa 2017). As French social historian Alain Corbin once wrote:

> The nose, as the vanguard of the sense of taste, warns us against poisonous substances. Even more important, the sense of smell locates hidden dangers in the atmosphere. Its capacity to test the properties of air is unmatched. (1986, 7)

Lucia, an activist from Naples, Italy, explained that she started to be involved in the struggles against toxic waste because she could no longer bear the stench invading her home (Lucia 2007). Nunzia, another activist from Naples, describes vividly what the stink can do to one's own body:

> As I was getting nearer to the fence, my throat was burning more and more, but not only the throat, also the eyes, the face, I felt pervaded by the stench, it was not only an olfactory sensation anymore. The smell was becoming more intense, the air thicker and cloudier, suffocating. It seemed as if I was not only smelling with the nose and the mouth, but also with my skin which was soaked with that stench, with those substances. ... I came back home and jumped in the shower, the smell was following me everywhere, I was soaked

in that stench to the bones. I was scratching my skin with the sponge, trying to erase that smell which was pervading me, but it did not go away. I looked devastated, with my face red and eyes swollen with tears and then again that smell, still with me. (Lombardi 2014, 31–32)

Nunzia's story confirms that the nose can act as a third eye, rendering the hidden map of the Wasteocene visible, while the stench reveals on which side of the wasting line one lives. For Miriam, another activist from Naples, the stench marks the invisible border between the two sides of the Wasteocene:

Coming close to some areas between the cities of Naples and Caserta means to feel sick and throw up. There is a pestilential stench like a punch in your stomach. (Corongiu 2017)

Narratively speaking, every conversion needs some kind of climax, a revealing experience which breaks the norm and opens up for an alternative self. Nonetheless, I argue that the smell is more than a rhetorical tool in the making of a rebellious self-narrative. Placing the nose at the center of the political reminds us that subaltern people experience the Wasteocene through their own bodies. The Wasteocene logic is, after all, embodied in the very texture of human and nonhuman life. The nose also questions the strict separation between experience and knowledge, thus proposing multiple ways to cognize the Wasteocene. As Rosa and Antonio, two Portuguese activists, argue, in wasted communities only official ways of gathering data and producing knowledge count; any other way of knowing is not considered. It is wasted, precisely as the people producing it (Pinto & Pratas 2017).

3.3 Wasteocene, Global and Local

Everywhere, wasted communities engage in some forms of guerrilla narrative, resisting the imposition of toxic narratives and the domestication of memories. It is thanks to these practices that many wasted stories have been salvaged, slowly sabotaging the mainstream narratives which hide the Wasteocene violence. Before moving in the next section of this Element to a close analysis – almost at the microscope – of the Wasteocene, I would like to make a bird's eye tour of our wasted planet pointing at few hotspots where wasting relationships leak and become visible against invisibilization and normalization.

A World Bank report – nothing more distant from guerrilla of any form – foresees that by 2050 the annual production of municipal solid waste will increase from 2.01 to 3.40 billion tonnes (Kaza et al. 2018, 3). According to World Bank analysts – and common sense – the more a country becomes richer, the more its production of waste will grow. As David Pellow (2002, 1) has reminded us, the poor may live among waste, but they are not the main producers of that waste. Someone else dumps it on them. The report also reminds us that waste is quite a vague label, since different economic systems produce different kinds of waste: more food and organic waste in low-and-middle-income countries (circa 50 percent) in comparison with that produced in affluent societies (30 percent) (Kaza et al. 2018, 17). The disparities in the distribution of waste has always attracted the World Bank; in a 1991 internal memo, the WB seemed to propose the relocation of polluting industries in the Global South in order to profit from the cheap costs of workers and their lives. Applying the Wasteocene logic by the book, the memo stated loud and clear that the wellbeing of the few must be based on the wasting of the Others. As historian Iris Borowy has written, the author of the memo tried to defend himself arguing that he had actually been sarcastic against the economists' blind faith in the free market (Borowy 2019). Unfortunately for the World Bank, that defensive argument did not work out and the 1991 internal memo became the ultimate demonstration of the imperial attitude of the Global North in terms of toxic waste. That memo, together with the infamous Cerrell report (1984), which advised the government of California to place waste facilities in poor and non-White communities, brutally proved the main point of this Element: the Wasteocene is not mainly a matter of waste but of wasting relationships aiming to produce disposable others.

While every kind of waste is a nuisance for those living close to it, toxic waste brings the level of harm to critical points. It is quite difficult to gather reliable data on toxic waste on a global scale because of the shifting definitions of what is "toxic," often varying from nation to nation, the invisibility of a large part of its flows, running through illegal channels, and the creative destruction of industrial capitalism, continuously introducing new substances (Bonneuil & Fressoz 2017, 54; Langston 2011, 17). According to the independent website Theworldcounts.com, every second 13 tons of hazardous waste are produced worldwide; almost 60 kilos for every human on the planet. The same website informs us that in seventy years, from the 1930s to the 2000s, the production of chemical substances has grown from 1 million to 400 million tons. A 2019 UN report confirmed the concerns of this independent website. The UN Special Rapporteur Baskut Tuncak gathered a considerable amount of data on the spread of toxic contamination in the world and its effects on human health. Quoting an article published in *The Lancet*,[11] the UN report stated that in 2015 about 9 million people died because of pollution, confirming toxic contamination as the "single largest source of premature death in the world today" (Tuncak 2019, 6). Just a few years before the publication of this UN special

---

[11] The article in question was Landrigan et al. 2018.

report, the World Health Organization produced quite an extensive "global assessment of the burden of disease from environmental risks" (Prüss-Ustün et al. 2016). According to the WHO, in 2012, more than 12 million deaths (23 percent of the total deaths) were caused by environmental problems (Prüss-Ustün et a. 2016, x). The same report stated that "out of the 133 diseases or disease groups listed in the Global Health Observatory . . ., 101 had significant links with the environment" (11), confirming that the wasting of the environment comes hand in hand with the wasting of people. Using data from a 2010 WHO report, the Green Cross Switzerland and Blacksmith Institute argued that more than 200 million people in the world were at risk of exposure to toxic pollution (Blacksmith Institute 2013, 5). The Blacksmith Institute report proceeded precisely in the same direction that I am going to propose, that is, shifting from aggregate data to the stories of specific hotspots, basically mapping the Wasteocene. I am not claiming any scientificity in the selection of the hotspots; without any doubt, mine is a personal selection, although I have attempted to represent the diversity of possible cases.

One does not need any sophisticated methodologies to guess that living in Cancer Alley, Louisiana, is like witnessing the everyday making of the Wasteocene. Surely the local authorities give that stretch of land the more reassuring name of Industrial Corridor, yet sometimes the tricks of toxic narratives do not work and a name cannot domesticate the rage and suffering coming from the material toxicity of "seven oil refineries and 136 petrochemical facilities" (Davies 2018, 1541) all packed in quite a small area between New Orleans and Baton Rouge. Indeed, the result is an appalling incidence of cancer and other diseases, which many residents and experts connect to the petrochemical industry. Quoting data from the United Health Foundation, the geographer Thom Davies reminds us that Louisiana has ranked among the worst US states in terms of public health, with "10,614 years of potential life lost before the age of seventy-five per 100,000 people" (Davies 2018, 1542). Data is powerful, of course, but perhaps stories even more so. Barbara Allen, who has provided a fundamental account of Cancer Alley, has rightly stressed the centrality of collective narratives as ways of knowing and making sense of the environment which is alternative to corporate or scientific discourses (2003, 20–21). One of those stories is that of Eugene and Joyce Willis, who moved from New Orleans to the rural community of St. Gabriel in a quest for a better environment to raise their children in (Baurick & Meiners 2019). They could not be more wrong about their decision: Joyce died in her early 40s from kidney problems and cancer. Living in Cancer Alley means to experience the Wasteocene to its extreme. There, the othering logic, which orders life and death, worth and insignificance, is rooted in the layers of racism embedded into the plantation economy. As Davies persuasively writes, the "conversion of former plantations into chemical plants created a distinctly discriminatory distribution of toxic risks and contributed to a form of environmental racism," described by Robert Bullard as "petrochemical colonialism" (Davies 2018, 1541).

While slow violence is the distinctive trait of the Wasteocene in Cancer Alley, Rio Doce in Brazil seems to be the perfect example of the almost explosive violence of extractivism and its effects on humans and more than human health. In his Ph.D. dissertation, Giuseppe Orlandini (2018/2019) describes the dam disaster of Mariana, starting from November 5, 2015 when the Fundão Dam collapsed releasing circa 50 million cubic meters of mineral waste mixed with mud. It has been considered the largest mining dam disaster in terms of magnitude of the toxic waste released, the affected area (the mud running through the entire river for 600 km), and the economic damage (more than 5 billion dollars) (Milanez & Losekann 2016, 11). The precise casualty figure can be questionable, but we know for sure that nineteen people were killed while "the interwoven ecological and socio-economic impacts [of the disaster] have affected hundreds of thousands of people in 41 cities across the Doce River basin" (Fernandes et al. 2016, 35). Indeed, the river was the first victim of this mining disaster; as stated clearly in a documentary about this event, there is no doubt that Rio Doce is dead (Costa 2015). The Wasteocene logic unites humans and nonhumans in its production of wasted lives and places. An entire ecosystem was subjugated to the mining industry under the usual extractivist regime which produces the ultimate other, disposable places and people to be exploited up to their exhaustion. The collapse of the dam was, of course, an extreme event, but it must be understood not as something exceptional, but rather as the manifestation of the Wasteocene "normal." As the Rede National de Médicas e Médicos Populares [National Networks of Grassroots Medical Doctors] has argued, the mining industries had already impacted the ecosystem and the people living there, even before the dam disaster, especially in relation to the access to clean and sufficient water supply (Rodrigues et al. 2016, 177). Another research proves that three years before the collapse of the dam, local people already feared a possible major disaster while lamenting the contamination of water and the continuous assault against their properties (Zhouri et al. 2017, 8). The collapse of the dam was only emblematic of the wider and older processes described decades ago by Edoardo Galeano in his masterpiece *Open Veins of Latin America*:

> Latin America is the region of open veins. Everything, from the discovery until our times, has always been transmuted into European – or later United States – capital . . .. Everything: the soil, its fruits and its mineral-rich depths,

the people and their capacity to work and to consume, natural resources and human resources. (1997, 2)

Galeano was writing about the manifold manifestations of Western extractivism in Latin America, a well-oiled machinery in the Wasteocene arsenal producing wasted people and places. Be it the gold miners of the Conquistadores or the rubber plantations of the Yankees, those wasting relationships extracted profits from the very life of humans and ecosystems. The immense e-waste dump of Agbogbloshie in Ghana is another type of open vein, one where the consumption of the rich and the waste lives of the poor meet. Indeed, nothing better than Agbogbloshie could embody the Wasteocene logic.

In 2013 the Blacksmith Institute and the Green Cross listed Agbogbloshie among the ten most toxic areas on the planet. More than 200,000 tons of secondhand electronic goods arrive every year to that dump, mostly from Western Europe (Heacock et al. 2016, 550). Giving a number for the people working in Agbogbloshie is a rather tentative exercise; according to the EJAtlas, the most accurate Environmental Justice world map,[12] the data fluctuates between 4,500–7,500 up to 10,000 (Petricca, Moloo, and Stoisser 2020). A report of the International Labor Organization relates that in Ghana 25,000 people work in the e-waste sector, which then supports up to 200,000 people (Lundgren 2012, 28). Those workers are exposed to several hazards coming from the general unhygienic conditions of the dump, the ways in which they disassemble the electronics, and the chemical properties of the materials – in other words, they are affected by the Wasteocene logic which disposes of both unwanted objects and unworthy people. The practice of extracting metals by burning household appliances is especially harmful to the workers, considering that "copper is a catalyst for dioxin formation and copper electrical wiring is coated with chlorine-containing polyvinyl chloride (PVC) plastic which also contributes to the formation of dioxins" (Lundgren 2012, 19). Data and scientific studies give an idea of Agbogbloshie, but pictures and videos can be more powerful tools to visualize the physical materialization of the Wasteocene[13]. Black smoke in the sky, metal scrap everywhere, cows grazing in the rubbish, and an army of humans working to extract values from someone else's waste – these are the main components in the documentaries and photographic reportages on Agbogbloshie. The stories of the children working in the dump are especially touching. While I do appreciate the power of those visual

---

[12] The EJAtlas is the largest open-access global database on environmental conflicts, ideated and coordinated by Joan Martinez Alier.

[13] See, for instance: Valentino Bellini's visual project www.bitrotproject.com/; Muntaka Chasant's collection of images at www.muntaka.com/agbogbloshie-e-waste/; and Artyom Somov's video documentary ToxiCity.

investigations – my writing will never offer such a vivid representation of Agbogbloshie – I fear that they may also somehow reinforce the othering perception resting beneath the Wasteocene logic. What might be missing from those visual narratives are the connections between Agbogbloshie and the rest, the flows of capitals and materials, the politics of land grabbing, expropriation, and expulsion of people that creates the army of dispossessed workers squeezing money out of waste. Finally, those visual narratives might buttress the sense that the Wasteocene is something occurring far away from us; but this is simply one of the pillars of the Wasteocene logic: the (re)production of wasted people and places serves the purpose to create a safe and worthy "we." But this is just a trick of the elites: the Wasteocene is everywhere and the safe and worthy "we" is always narrowing its borders. The Wasteocene is not over there, it is here.

4 The Wasteocene at the Microscope

4.1 A City with a View on the Wasteocene: Sick Naples

The Wasteocene is embodied, material, carnal. As much as the Anthropocene seems abstract and global, the Wasteocene always reorients us toward the specificities of places, stories, and people. Do not get me wrong, though. The Wasteocene is a deeply planetary phenomenon both in scope and contents. Nonetheless, it serves better than other narratives to reveal how much those global issues are intertwined with particular bodies, ecologies, and stories. I did not theorize the Wasteocene. I have lived through it. I have seen it. I have smelled and breathed it. I am from it. Naples, in the South of Italy, has long been considered one of the many gates into the Wasteocene. The ancient Romans believed that the doors of the Inferno were just outside Naples, in the Averno Lake, even if sometimes I have wondered on which side of the door the Inferno was actually lurking from.

For being a city in the Global North, Naples is an odd object; indeed, it has often been perceived as a space in between, neither modern nor poor enough to claim a definitive and exclusive identity. Waste and dirtiness have always been crucial parts of such an uncertain identity. While I am writing these lines, the city is again experiencing one of its cyclical waste crises, though milder than the 2000s one, when almost the entire world witnessed the manifestation of the Wasteocene in the city streets of Naples. Articles on the garbage crisis in Campania – the region around Naples – appeared in the *Newsweek*, *The New York Times*, *The Economist*, *El Pais*, *Le Monde*, and *The Guardian*, while the websites of CNN, BBC, and Al Jazeera all contain reports on Naples and waste. However, the blending of waste and Naples goes far beyond the recent stories from the last decades. In the last couple of centuries, Naples has been a large open-air laboratory, analyzed by scientists and intellectuals, an archetype of unsolved problems and home of social and political experiments. Arriving in Naples, those travelers often turned into more or less improvised sociologists, delighted to give their explanations on the conditions of the city and its inhabitants. Sometimes, those travelers did have some extraordinary intuitions as Walter Benjamin's "porous city," which Serenella Iovino has reinterpreted as a metaphor of the metabolism linking Naples and its inhabitants (Iovino 2016, 13–46).

Then came the real investigations, usually stimulated by the string of epiphanies unveiling the wasted nature of the city and its inhabitants. Epidemics were always a clear break into the Wasteocene, they shouted loud and clear that bodies, power, and waste were connected through socio-ecological relationships. While John Scanlan argues that garbage can "reveal an alternative truth about how things really were" (2005, 136), I believe that breaks such as epidemics in the Wasteocene normality can uncover the truth about wasting relationships.

The cholera epidemics of 1884 and 1973 were the epiphanies of the Wasteocene, the revealing moments confirming not simply the dirtiness of the city but its deep otherness. Only a few years before the 1884 cholera epidemic, the Italian writer and artist Renato Fucini published his reportage from Naples, describing the city as a place radically diverse from civilized Europe. Fucini explicitly associated Naples to the Orient, arguing that the narrowness of the streets, the poverty of people, and the filth everywhere could easily deceive the travelers, convincing them to be in Alexandria in Egypt rather than in a European city (Fucini 1878, 4). He makes the point explicitly clear a few pages later, where he states that Naples was one of the dirtiest cities in Europe (14). During the same years, the English writer and philanthropist Jessie White Mario (1877) was also denouncing the horrific conditions in which the poor were forced to live in Naples. Her book, with the unequivocal title *La Miseria di Napoli* [The misery of Naples], was full of sick bodies immersed within dirty environments. Visiting the abysmal shelters were the poor lived – caves, basements, *bassi*[14], or dilapidated rooms – almost inevitably White Mario placed at the center of the scene a sick child, someone affected by typhus laying on a straw bed, or an emaciated mother struggling to feed her newborns. In her exposé of Naples' misery, the Wasteocene seems to be materialized distinctly through the trans-corporeal connections linking wasted people and wasted places. The fact that her book focused on the poor removes any doubt about

---

[14] Bassi are one-room apartments opening directly on the street through the entrance door which also acts as the only opening in the entire apartment.

the nature of the relationships producing wasted people and places; those are socio-ecological relationships (re)producing social injustices and not just urban aberrations of a premodern city. Writing during the 1884 cholera epidemics, the writer and journalist Matilde Serao described what she called "the bowels of Naples" as a place soaked up in waste, where all the modern barriers separating humans and their daily spaces from the impure were erased. In a detailed research on the 1884 and 1911 cholera epidemics, the historian Frank Snowden confirmed those arguments. As he writes. "cholera is an infallible indicator of destitution and squalor, of overcrowded dwellings and sanitary neglect, of defective sewers and unwashed hands" (1995, 16). However, those environmental conditions were amplified by poverty, or, using our language, by the socio-ecological relationships which made some parts of the city and its inhabitants disposable (30). Poverty, waste, and contamination were the pillars of this Neapolitan political ecology of epidemics, indeed, the historical materi-alization of the Wasteocene.

The epidemics, as any other spectacular emergency, offer a special view of the Wasteocene, because while the usual wasting of people and places is normalized and invisibilized, those exceptional situations impose looking for "solutions." But those solutions only aim to restore the Wasteocene norm rather than changing it completely. This is not so different from the Anthropocene discourse and the reification of CO_2 emissions: searching for the solution to "the thing" does not imply dismantling the socio-ecological relationships which have created "the thing" in the first place.

The 1884 cholera epidemic works as a handbook example of this discourse. As always with the Wasteocene, placing the blame on the victims is a crucial dispositif for controlling the emergency while keeping intact the underlying norms. The Neapolitan poor were part of the contaminated ecologies producing the epidemic. The dirtiness around them permeated both their bodies and souls, producing degraded communities, sick beyond the actual biological contagion. The problem was not to revert wasting relationships but to control them, to be sure that the othering order they were supposed to impose would not explode, blurring the borders between the designed social dumps and the rest. As in a well-oiled script, the reaction to the 1884 cholera epidemic was the imple-mentation of an urban policy designed to reinstall the borders between wasted and clean, pure and impure. Visiting the lower neighborhoods of the city, the Italian Prime Minister Agostino Depretis pronounced a phrase soon to become the motto of Neapolitan sanitization: "Naples must be gutted." The metaphor of the bowels seemed especially effective in describing the sick body of Naples. In the Neapolitan Wasteocene, the bowels of people and those of the city were intertwined through a dirtiness that spilled over, transforming everything and everyone into a socio-ecological dump. More than a surgical metaphor or a medical prescription, gutting the bowels of Naples seemed to be a declaration of war; and such a war was not only – perhaps not even mainly – against the Cholera vibrio and the wasted districts where it had flourished. I argue that the sanitization policy following the 1884 cholera epidemic targeted mainly the subaltern people living in the most degraded areas of the city. Those people and their dilapidated houses had to leave to make room for modern buildings for the middle class. A large, Haussmann-style boulevard[15] trenched the overcrowded and poor areas where the epidemic was particularly rugged; and yet on neither side of this boulevard had the situation changed. The construction of an aristocratic boulevard and of middle-class housing compressed the livable space for the poor even more. With more than thirty-five thousand destitute inhabitants expelled from the sanitized districts, the sanitization policy following the 1884 cholera epidemic meant deportation on a massive scale. While the cholera epidemic risked blowing up the othering infrastructures securing the immunization of the rich and the disposability of the poor, the consequent measures were meant to restructure the wasting relationships while hiding their crude consequences. Frank Snowden confirms the structural limits of the emergency intervention in the aftermath of the epidemics. Building upon a rich variety of sources, he has no doubt in arguing that "[a]ll of the symptoms of urban pathology targeted by the great renewal project were still present, including the marked disparities between the Upper and Lower Cities." (1995, 221). The 1884 cholera epidemic unveiled the Wasteocene in the most dramatic way. Wasting relationships had produced wasted places and wasted people, dividing the urban space between the clean and healthy districts of the middle-upper classes and the polluted and sick environments of the poor. However, the explosion of the epidemic questioned the foundational order of the Wasteocene, that is, the othering project, which was supposed to build a safe "us" against a contaminated and threatening "them." Gutting the bowels of Naples was a restoration of the Wasteocene order rather than a radical change of it.

A confirmation of this lies in the fact that after the 1884 cholera, the city experienced other epidemics, some almost invisible, in the pure Wasteocene style, others spectacular or perhaps spectacularized. I was seven years old when my parents took me to get the anti-cholera vaccination. It was 1973 and Naples was exposed, again, to a cholera outbreak, proving the city's uncertainty in belonging to the modern and immunized world once more. The only memories I have of that period is the unbearable amount of lemons that my

---

[15] In the second half of the nineteenth century, Georges-Eugène Haussmann was in charge of a large urban renovation project in Paris which included the transformation of the ancient narrow alleys in wide boulevards, easier to control in case of insurgencies.

father forced us to eat – apparently this was a good prevention of the disease – and the almost compulsive fear of any kind of street food and seafood, which I might add still accompanies me to this day. It is not clear how many people were killed by this late epidemic in Naples, perhaps around twenty. Almost one thousand were hospitalized, mostly not actually sick but overwhelmed by fear. The first recorded case was in a town outside Naples, Torre Annunziata, and more specifically in a narrow alley with the telling name of St. Joseph's marshes [San Giuseppe alle paludi]. Of course, there is no relationship between cholera and marshes; all the clues actually point to the mussels, and most probably, some specific mussels imported from Tunisia, where the epidemic had already spread. The truth is that the Cholera vibrio, that is, the pathogenic agent responsible for the epidemic, was never found in the Neapolitan mussels, nevertheless, the amount of contamination discovered in the clams was so high that the authorities decided to dismantle the nurseries in the sea around the city. In an interview, the coroner entrusted by the public prosecutors of Naples to discover the origins of the epidemic declared:

> At the time, a concentration of four coli bacteria per gram of mussel was accepted [by the sanitary authorities]. I had to note that in the Neapolitan mussels the coli bacteria per gram of mussel were 400,000! The paradoxical thing was that the mussels hosted such a concentrate of coli bacteria, due to the pollution of the sea, that even the Cholera vibrio would not survive in them. In short, there was cholera in Naples, but the notorious Cholera vibrio was never found. (Lambiase & Zappalà 2007)

Once again, the epidemic pulled off the invisibilization and normalization of Wasteocene relationships, revealing more systemic and persistent structures. Indeed, already in 1970, Naples registered higher percentages of stillbirths, child mortality and infectious diseases than the national averages (Chubb 1980).[16] On Sunday September 9, 1973, the radical left newspaper *Lotta Continua* reported on the front page the death of the eighteen-month-old Francesca Noviello. For them, it was well clear, since the very title of the article (*What killed Francesca was not only cholera*), that the cholera was not the only culprit for her death. In fact, the Noviello family lived in a dilapidated building under completely unsanitary conditions. To add injury to insult, the entire family, including Francesca, were left without any precautionary control even after the father was hospitalized because he was infected by the epidemic. *Lotta Continua* reported that after Francesca's death, the other families living in the same building

---

[16] 23.6/1,000 stillbirths and 58.9/1,000 deaths in the first year of life, in contrast to national. infectious tious diseases reached a level of 33.8/1,000, in contrast to a national average of 8.3/1,000.

began rioting, obtaining to be relocated temporarily in a high school (Lotta Continua 1973b). Though with a language and rhetoric which seem so far away from our times, *Lotta Continua* offered a profound interpretation of the epidemic as the tip of an iceberg of unjust socio-ecological relationships producing wasting people and places. Glossing a scientific explanation of the epidemic *Lotta Continua* wrote:

> This long scientific exposition repeats the simple truth that the proletarians of Naples have been saying since they began their fight against cholera: that the whole city, well beyond the mussel farms of St. Lucia, is for them a permanent breeding ground of infection. Permanent, as are all the cities built by and for the capitalists. (Lotta Continua 1973a)

I could not find any statistics about the precise geographical distribution of the 1973 cholera epidemic in the metropolitan area of Naples. One scientific paper, published a year after the epidemic, offered information about the social status of cholera patients; out of the ninety-six who were interviewed, a large majority were either unemployed or had manual jobs (Baine et al. 1974, 1372). In the 1970s, Naples was definitely a city marked dramatically by poverty. After all, in 1979, six years after the cholera epidemic, Naples was shocked by another highly controversial public health emergency. Called by the media, "the dark disease," a respiratory illness began to affect a large number of Neapolitan children. The history of the dark disease is too controversial to be summarized in a few lines; certainly, it has manifold aspects including issues connected to the politics of public health and of the media. Nonetheless, I employ this example within my theoretical framework of the Wasteocene; for me, the dark disease reinforces my argument of a city where periodic crises shed light on systemic and long-lasting wasting relationships producing others, disposable subjects living in socio-ecological dumps. In the same year, a coalition of grassroots organizations, unions, and militant experts published a pamphlet on the origins of the disease, which gave voice to the socio-environmental justice argument about the children's epidemic (Coordinamento Provinciale Salute et al. 1979). Without too many frills, the authors of the pamphlet connected the explosion of this respiratory disease to poverty, stressing the ordinariness of a socio-ecological condition which pushed the child death rate in some districts up to 135 per thousand. The mainstream narrative loved to speak of a "dark" disease, hinting at some mystery to be solved, while all the counter-hegemonic narratives of the event stressed the normality of it. The front page of the newspaper of the Italian Communist Party *l'Unità* published an article by one of the party cadres with the unequivocal title "There is nothing unknown (dark) about the Neapolitan dark disease" (Geremicca 1979). While *l'Unità* concentrated its energies on defending the leftist municipal government of the city, the authors of the pamphlet, coming from the radical left, articulated a more compelling narrative about what was occurring in Naples. First of all, they made clear that the so-called "dark disease" was selective in its killing by "choosing the marginalized, those forced to live in the *bassi* and excluded from all types of health information" (Coordinamento provinciale salute 1979, 4). For them, the exploitation of those marginal subjects reached a point in which the very reproduction of the workforce was not included within the capitalistic extraction of value:

> Here people are almost cannon fodder. The point is not only to exploit their labor force; their lives are stolen, through an intensive and massive exploitation. (2)

A few lines below, the pamphlet pointed to the hazardous conditions in which children – mainly girls – were forced to work in the illegal leather factories, being exposed to the toxicity of chemical glues every day. Their conclusions could easily be my own conclusions, since they resonate shockingly close to my thinking on the essence of the Wasteocene; as soon as the toxicity made those working girls unable to produce, "they were disposed of as used objects, waste" (2).

This coalition of grassroots organizations, unions, and militant experts bridged the public health crisis with the wasting relationships that produced subaltern bodies destined to be disposable since birth. The vexation they felt toward those they called the "vampires of piety" is similar to my own vexation toward those who are lamenting the coming ecological crisis and asking for a collective effort. What is missing in both cases is a reflection on the causes of the crisis, whatever it might be, and a too comfortable demand for a postfact solidarity, one which does not challenge the wasting relationships of the Wasteocene but only mitigates/invisibilizes them.

Those counter-hegemonic narratives revealed the reality of the Wasteocene beyond the points of fracture represented by the epidemics. Because the Wasteocene does not manifest itself only through the climactic fractures of epidemics but also through the daily hell in which the poor are forced to live. The Neapolitan waste emergency truly serves to reveal this mundane Wasteocene.

4.2 The Wild Waste West

In January 2008 a large area on the west side of Naples radically changed its landscape. Checkpoints, barricades, and burnt public buses offered a warlike image which one would not expect in that part of the world. An entire town – Quarto, 40,000 inhabitants – and several neighborhoods in the city of Naples were completely sealed; nothing and nobody could enter or exit from those areas. As if a city under siege, people experienced the scarcity of primary goods and only for exceptional reasons were they authorized to pass with their cars through checkpoints. Therefore, when the mayor of Quarto launched an appeal to police and protesters to open a humanitarian corridor for the inhabitants of his town, nobody was too surprised; evidently, this kind of military language seemed appropriate for the situation. Indeed, people were suddenly hurled into a landscape of war, the war of garbage. The great riot of Pianura against the reopening of the largest and oldest landfill of the region is the entry point of my exploration into what I have called the mundane Wasteocene.

Although the dirtiness of this Southern Italian city has always been a characteristic mark of its hybrid identity, nonetheless, the so-called waste emergency of the 1990s and 2000s represents a landmark in this history of wasting relationships. I argue that the waste crisis is another fracture into the toxic narratives that normalize/invisibilize the Wasteocene, and not because of the trash bags overflooding the streets of Naples – the waste pornography so loved by mainstream media and scholars – but because it reveals the unjust socio-ecological relationships establishing who and what have value.

The Neapolitan waste emergency has in itself a long history: it officially began in 1994, when criminal investigations revealed the inadequacy of the landfills operating in the region, seizing most of them. With only a few functioning dumps, the waste started to overflow in the streets of Naples, inducing the national government to declare a state of emergency which led to the creation in 1994 of a special agency for the management of waste (the Commissariat for the Waste Emergency in Campania – CWEC). This agency deprived local elected bodies of their authority while entrusting the solution of the waste crisis to technocrats with exceptional resources and power. Several scholars, including myself, have framed the Neapolitan waste crisis as a crisis of democracy (Iovino 2009; D'Alisa et al. 2010; Armiero & D'Alisa 2012; Berruti & Palestino 2020); the very idea of an emergency – though a peculiar one lasting for almost twenty years – implied the implementation of special measures, not subjected to the normal norms and procedures. This is a key feature of the Wasteocene as a system producing unjust arrangements of socio-ecological relationships. Giorgio Agamben (2010) and Naomi Klein (2008), though with different angles, have both explained how capitalism continuously reproduces itself through the creation of states of exception which accelerate the othering processes as means of capitalist accumulation. As with the renewal of the city following the 1884 cholera epidemic (the Risanamento), also the waste emergency regime aimed to solve "the problem," rather than addressing its causes and social ramifications. If the problem was the trash in the streets – especially in the posh areas of the city – the solution had to be to find places where the waste could be disposed of. The enforcement of an emergency regime never fosters a revolutionary plan, it is not meant to implement radical progressive changes but more likely it is designed to reproduce the status quo. In other words, an emergency regime serves to restore the othering order of the Wasteocene, not to dismantle it.

Thinking of the 1990s-2000s waste crisis in terms of a Wasteocene epiphany means to go beyond the narrow emergency created with the foreclosure of several, more or less legal, landfills in 1994. Let me repeat once more that my idea of the Wasteocene does not coincide with heaps of garbage on the street. Of course, these are not a pleasant feature of the urban landscape and, generally, they do manifest the socio-ecological injustices entrenched in the organization of the urban space. Indeed, as Martin Melosi has reminded us, historically, a working-class neighborhood has always been more likely to be dirty than the financial district or an upper-class area (Melosi 2005, 2694 ebock). What the Wasteocene does to this state of affairs is to normalize it through a toxic narrative that blames the victims while naturalizing the socio-ecological relationships producing wasted people and places. Too often, pointing at the waste in the streets implies to be blind to the manifold invisible connections that produce the waste in the first place, and to enforce the borders between dirty and clean, antiseptic and contaminated. Removing the trash bags from the streets can be a perfect mechanism of the Wasteocene: if waste is matter out of place, restoring the order by confining it to the space where it belongs is nothing less than reproducing the Wasteocene. In the Neapolitan waste emergency, this meant to transform subaltern communities in socio-ecological dumps where waste infrastructures were added upon preexisting contaminations; waste added upon waste, precisely as Charles Mills has brilliantly argued in his *Black Trash* (Mills 2001, 89).

A large part of the work of the special agency for the waste emergency entailed finding places for the storage/disposal of urban garbage. In the name of the emergency, the CWEC could violate European, national, and regional rules and procedures, including environmental impact assessment. Several criminal investigations have proved that the temporary storage places opened by the CWEC often did not comply with the minimal standards for environmental safety. Those measures aimed at restoring the fundamental rules of the Wasteocene: sorting out wasted and cleaned, impeding the spilling of wasted matter outside the designed zones, and reproducing social dumps for the confinement of the unwanted.

For a large part, the Neapolitan waste crisis was a sort of carousel, with the CWEC working to clean the city streets, moving the trash somewhere else, and the communities where that trash was supposed to end up pushing back against this. Often, it seemed easier to target rural communities with few inhabitants and weaker political and social resources. Sometimes the decisions taken by the special agency were clearly absurd, as, for instance, in 2007, when they tried to open a gigantic landfill – Valle della Masseria – a stone's throw away from a nature protection park, potentially affecting the hydrographic basin of the Sele River. The following year was the turn of a small village in the inland of the region, Sant'Arcangelo a Trimonte, designed to contain up to 7500 tons of waste. In 2010 the CWEC planned to open the largest landfill of Europe in the Vesuvius National Park – Cava Vitiello – with a storage capacity of ten million tons of waste (Ciccone 2010). The assumption that those rural communities were easier to tame did not always work as foreseen. Both Valle della Masseria and Cava Vitiello landfills could not be completed and put to work, at least not as they were initially designed, because of the strenuous opposition of local inhabitants. Isolation and having a scarce population were not the only golden rules for the selection of areas for waste storage and infrastructures. It was quite common that new landfills and other waste facilities were planned to be built in the proximity of existing dumps or in areas already affected by contamination. As the ordering principle of the Wasteocene is to reproduce privilege through the wasting of subaltern communities, it makes sense to reinforce the existing socio-ecological inequalities. Areas affected by illegal dumping, as in the Vesuvius, or by almost-legal landfills became the ideal locations for new waste facilities. For instance, both Valle della Masseria and Cava Vitiello were very close to preexisting landfills, while a brand-new incinerator was built in a community already marked by industrial contamination. Indeed, often the communities resisted the construction of waste facilities in their territory campaigning under the slogan "We have already pulled our weight" [abbiamo già dato].[17] Similarly, in the haste of the continuous emergency – i.e. the heaps of trash in the streets – the CWEC resolved to reopen landfills which had already been closed, waiting for reclamation.

This was the case of Pianura, the working-class neighborhood I have evoked in the opening of this section. In 2008, the CWEC decided to reopen the Pianura landfill which had been closed in 1998 with the promise to be reclaimed. Pianura had hosted the older and, for a long time, larger landfill of the region; within the perimeter of Naples, it was the neighborhood of waste, a community deeply marked by the presence of the dump. In the 1950s, when the landfill was opened, Pianura was still a rural area, close enough to the city to be used as a handy dump for the growing metropolitan area. As a perfect Wasteocene hotspot, Pianura became the terminal for all the unwanted remnants of the modern city, both humans and nonhuman. Growing up in the 1970s in a more or less middle-class neighbourhood in Naples, I can still remember the shocking experiences of visiting some relatives living in Pianura. It was truly a trip into another world. Leaving the parts of the city which were familiar to me, I can recollect feeling as if I was entering an environment which was not still. At the time, Pianura seemed like a gigantic and confusing construction site where everything looked half finished and half not. Nevertheless, some people, including my relatives, lived in that world in progress, often literally living door to door with skeletons of homes which left me wondering whether they were abandoned or not. After all, this was the way in which Pianura worked: everything had to be built up quickly, sometimes in one night, and it had to look inhabited in order for it not to be demolished by the authorities. In the 70s, Pianura was the urban frontier; it looked like our wild west with pioneers, half heroes, half outlaws, moving into a space deprived of the urban services normal to any city, even Naples. Instead, there were several rather unusual things: too many street dogs, large greenfields, and a stench that pervaded everything in the neighborhood. At the time when I was visiting my relatives in Pianura, I did not comprehend the urban ecologies of waste, and I could not make any connection between the poor conditions of the area and the fact that it had been selected as the ultimate dump for the entire region. The stink was just another reminder that Pianura was the "otherness"; the city I knew was over and another space was in place. This sensorial landscape of smell was a key detector that made visible the present the socio-ecological violence of the Wasteocene. While the so-called waste crisis forced the frontiers of the Wasteocene, bringing waste to the center of the metropolis, the Pianura stink remained stuck to the place and the people inhabiting it. It did not trespass the borders ordering the Wasteocene, on the contrary, it made those borders visible. Precisely as it occurred to me when I was visiting my relatives, the smell signaled the entrance into another zone, one deeply other from the immunized place I was from.

Something very similar occurred to Doriana, an activist fighting against the reopening of the Pianura landfill. In her memoirs about how she became an environmental activist, Doriana vividly described the impact of the big stench of Pianura. Coming from one of the posh neighborhoods of the city, Doriana had envisioned her moving to Pianura as a sort of going back to the countryside. With a group of friends, she had bought an old house there, imagining a bucolic life a stone's throw from the city. Doriana, however, realized the power of the dump over her life – and actually over the entire community where she had moved in – almost immediately:

> It was when we brought our furniture there that we started to feel it. The stink, the terrible, queasy, sweetish smell, which now is so familiar to me. This was

how we discovered that our house was at less than one kilometer as the crow
flies from the dump. (Sarli 2014, 103)

Reading Doriana's story is like reading the instruction manual for the Wasteocene.
Rule number 1: never leave the part of the world where you belong; rule number 2:
do not ask yourself where the unwanted remains of your wealth end up; rule
number 3: in case you meet the reality of the Wasteocene, just run away, do not try
to change it.

Although as an embodied experience the stink is deeply place-based, in the
case of Pianura it also travels across the borders of the Wasteocene, attached to
the identity of the people living there. As cruel as kids can be, I remember some
of my friends from the complex building where I used to live accusing my
cousins of smelling badly as soon as they knew they were from Pianura. In an
interview I have collected with one of the leaders of the 2008 protest, he stated
that the stink had always followed him, even outside of Pianura (Marco 2011).

The landfill worked for about forty years. During these years, the neighborhood
around the dump changed dramatically. The small rural area of the 1950s and 60s,
with a few thousand inhabitants, disappeared in the 1970s and 80s, when Pianura
was involved in a dramatic urban transformation. The 1980 earthquake worsened
the housing situation in Naples, especially in the historical center where several old
buildings became inhabitable, leaving many people without proper housing. The
illegal construction of houses in Pianura attracted thousands of people and the area
reached a population of about 60,000 inhabitants in 2001. While the population
was increasing, Pianura did not receive any public services; defined purely as the
neighborhood of the landfill, an identity that persists to this day. In fact, the 1950
landfill was progressively enlarged, reaching about 70 hectares. However, the
impact of the landfill on the neighborhood was not only a matter of dimension, it
also depended on the quality of the dump and its management. Until 1984, the
landfill was operated almost without any kind of technological measures in order
to minimize its environmental and health impacts. Moreover, the control over the
quality of the waste entering the landfill was not reassuring. Legally, the landfill
was meant to host only urban garbage, until in 1989 the local government allowed
the disposal of toxic and noxious waste.[18] Referring to legal investigations, the
Parliamentary Committee on the Waste Cycle stated that about 1,000 tons of
highly toxic sludge from the ACNA factory of Cengio – one of the most infamous
cases of industrial pollution in post WWII Italy – were dumped in the Pianura
landfill. It has also been proven that toxic ash from the thermoelectrical plants of

---

[18] An inventory of the materials dumped in the Pianura landfill was produced by the Provincial
government of Naples with a document dated 14 May 2008/2352; now this document is
published in Manzo & Musella 2012.

the Italian National Electric Power Company – that is, a state owned company until 1999 – has been dumped there. According to a document produced by the Provincial Government of Naples, from the 1980s to the 1990s, the landfill gathered all kinds of toxic waste, from biomedical waste to asbestos dust. The document mentions generic special waste weighing about 493,000,000 kilograms and more than 953,000,000 kilograms of different kinds of sludge (Provincia di Napoli 2008).

In 1996 the dump was closed; at the time Naples was living what has been pompously called the Neapolitan Renaissance, meaning a political season of extensive restyling of the urban environment and, above all, of its representa-tions led by a new and extremely popular mayor, Antonio Bassolino. The closing of the Pianura landfill and the promise to reclaim and transform it into a golf course were therefore part of that narrative about the general regeneration of the city. Unfortunately, as I have already said, no reclamation or golf course was implemented. Instead of reclaiming it, the area of Pianura remained extremely contaminated. According to the Sebiorec report,[19] in Pianura there is a statistically significant association between the proximity to dumps and the presence of dioxin and furans (PCDD and PCDF) in the blood (Sebiorec 2010). Other reports speak of conspicuous infiltration of leachate, leakage of biogas, and traces of dioxin in the leachate tank (Crescenti 2009).

The Wasteocene materialized in Pianura through the construction of a socio-ecological dump. Once again, it is clear that while the official discourse about the waste crisis aimed to speak merely of domestic trash, the reality of the Wasteocene was much more toxic and pervasive. Several sources refer to an extraordinary diffusion of cancer and other diseases in the area. Elisa, a Pianura resident I interviewed, offered a dramatic sequence of diseases: her husband had surgery for cancer, their son has been asthmatic since birth, and her sister-in-law died of cancer when she was forty. In his deposition in the trial for the riot of Pianura, Marco Nonno states that every family living in Contrada Pisani has at least one member sick with cancer and a child suffering from asthma (Trial Pianura 2011a). In the video reportage "Nelle Terre di Gomorra" [In Gomorrah Lands], Maria Candida, an inhabitant of Pianura, tells that her husband and son both died of cancer after they moved to a new house overlooking the landfill (De Simone et al. 2011).

Clearly this type of slow violence is difficult to trace, scientific knowledge is uncertain, and power inequalities make everything even more complicated since

---

[19] Sebiorec was a research project funded by the Campania regional government to investigate the presence of dioxin and heavy metals in human blood. There has also been a mystery connected with this project because for several months it was not released until a popular magazine was able to publish it (Fittipaldi 2011).

affected communities do not have the kind of resources needed to prove the causal connections between specific sources of toxicity and health issues. However, we should never underestimate the significance of slow violence which, while it might seem invisible to most people, is extremely present in the lives of those who have experienced it. Pianura is an extremely rich case study because it illustrates, almost graphically, the Wasteocene logic: the creation of a socio-ecological dump and the imposition of a slow violence regime on the lives and bodies of people confined there were accompanied by the exertion of the more visible violence of the state repressive apparatus. After all, maintaining structural violence for so long implies significant doses of direct violent repression; generally, people do not accept passively to be contaminated. Along with stories of illness, police violence is the other common trope present in almost all the memories of Pianura activists. In 2004, when the CWEC decided to reopen the landfill as a temporary waste storage, the inhabitants peacefully opposed the plan with the usual pickets and marches and they were violently repressed by the police. "We were beaten by the police while we were lying on the ground", explains Maria. Annamaria went through a trial because she tried to stop some trucks and she states clearly that after the 2004 traumatic experience everybody kept saying: "Next time, they [the police] will pay." Doriana recollects the police charging with tear gas against pacific demonstrators, including women and children.[20]

The connection between the slow violence of structural socio-ecological injustices and the open violence of police repression found a dramatic manifestation on January 10, 2011, in a court hearing for the 2008 riots of Pianura. A witness was passionately recollecting the 2004 repression against unarmed citizens when the judge interrupted his deposition arguing that it was time to forget such old stories (Pianura Trial 2011b). The man answered that his wife was sick with cancer and therefore he would never forget. I believe that this story effectively represents the Wasteocene logic and its violence. In the trial for the riot of Pianura, the state, impersonated by the judge, asked the victims to forget the violence perpetuated by the police against them simply because "time had passed." On the other hand, a witness, who endured the repression, affirmed his right to remember. Even more interesting to the understanding of the Wasteocene logic, the witness made a fascinating and apparently random connection between the violence perpetuated by the police and the sickness of his wife. The connection, however, is not arbitrary at all, but actually expresses the link between slow violence – that is, the environmental injustice embodied in the dump and in the body of the woman – and the violence deployed by the police. As a matter of fact, without the repressive apparatus it would be impossible to impose unequal distribution of risks on

---

[20] All these testimonies were collected during a focus group I held in Pianura.

marginal communities. Asking people to forget about the suffered violence while simultaneously judging the violence on the side of the protesters is rather emblematic of the Wasteocene logic: normalizing unjust socio-ecological relationships, justifying repressive violence, and concealing slow violence.

As the epidemics I have illustrated above, the waste crisis similarly exposes a crack in the usual choreography of the Wasteocene. The crisis made waste visible, bringing it to the core of city's social life, in its central and residential districts. The usual invisible flows of waste matter stopped working properly, hence breaking the borders that protect the clean "we" from the dirty "others." This process of the visibilization of waste and the spasmodic attempt to restore the internal borders of the Wasteocene also had another effect: they mobilized the communities which were on the receiving end of the waste flow. The crisis was then an opportunity to either reinstall the preexisting power relationships or to get rid of them entirely. The resilient paradigm suggests that a community is strong when it has the ability to go back to the precrisis condition, but I wonder whether this is always a desirable outcome.[21] If unjust socio-ecological relationships have produced the Wasteocene, creating social dumps and immunized communities, should we really aim to go back to them? Is resilience rather than resistance really a better strategy to exit the Wasteocene? The Wasteocene diaries from Naples speak not only of the injustices continuously (re)producing social dumps, but also of the resistance to those injustices. The waste crisis contributed to the politicization of issues and actors as it had never happened before. As Serenella Iovino has written:

> [T]he narrative agency of Naples's porous bodies conveys the matter and discourses of their formative histories. In so doing, this agency creates ties of awareness that, disclosing the processes at work in these bodies' becoming, restore their political imagination. (2016, 38)

In section 5, we will explore in detail how the embodied experience of the Wasteocene has the potential to create new political subjects who foster collective imaginaries to radically change the present.

5 Sabotaging the Wasteocene

5.1 Sharing the Bread and the Roses

While I was writing the section of this Element on science fiction and the waste apocalypse, I became critically ill. COVID-19 was already shattering the world, but it seemed a too distant reality from my suburban life in Stockholm. Sometimes the othering – like the divine providence – works in mysterious ways, and I ended

---

[21] On the ambiguities of the resilience paradigm see Kaika 2017.

up experiencing within my body the very material apocalypse that the pandemic had brought onto our lives. For my family and me, it was as if a weird apocalypse tore apart our otherwise comfortable lives. Now, months after my hospitalization, I see clearly that the pandemic did not actually waste our lives, and not only because I survived, evidently. COVID-19 is indeed a powerful manifestation of the Wasteocene; most likely, it arises from the erosion of available space for wildlife (Malm 2020, 35; 41) and, although it has badly hit countries in the Global North, several scholars have argued that ethnic minorities, working class people, and urban poor have paid/will pay a higher price for the pandemic, both within their bodies and from their pockets. For slum dwellers, the heartfelt appeals to stay at home and wash their hands seem to be either insults or jokes. In the United States, scholars have started to work on the correlation between the spread of the pandemic and ethnic minorities, recording higher rates of morbidity and death among African Americans, Latinx, and Native Americans (Patel et al. 2020; Shah et al. 2020). Considering I experienced COVID-19 in its deadliest form firsthand, it is true that epidemics may sometimes tear down the Wasteocene's seemingly impregnable walls between the disposable "them" and the valuable "us." Nevertheless, as I described in subsection 4.1 with the cholera epidemics in Naples, the Wasteocene logic will immediately repair the cracks in the walls, restoring the othering divide. I was lucky enough to be on the side of the dividing line which would guarantee me excellent medical care, family support, even an ambassador intervening in my favor, a comfortable house to come home to, and a salary every month. I know COVID-19 is terrible, I have lived it, but I also realize it may be more terrible for others than it has been for a white Italian professor living in Sweden.

As COVID-19 is yet another manifestation of the Wasteocene, it also offers a telling example of what I wish to discuss in this section 5, that is, the blooming of grassroots initiatives challenging the Wasteocene regime while prefiguring another world, one beyond wasting relationships and othering projects. Going back to the science fiction narratives where I had to stop writing, the return of barbarism and the end of civilization are almost always key tropes in those stories. In the case of global catastrophes, humans will start to kill each other, fighting to get control of the most precious resources, be them food, water, oil, or even books. *Homo homini lupus* – each man is a wolf for another man, this is the adage proposed by those narratives. Sometimes watching those apocalyptic movies, it seems to see, represented on the screen, Margaret Thatcher's gloomy words: "There is no such thing as society: there are individual men and women, and there are families." But the UK Prime Minister and the science fiction versions of her argument were actually wrong. Communities exist and in the most difficult moments they mobilize. As wasting relationships are based on consuming and othering, commoning practices aim to reproduce resources and communities and in doing so, they dismantle the othering project, create communities, and have the potential to undermine the Wasteocene regime.

During the COVID-19 pandemic, there has been much evidence to prove that Thatcher was wrong and commoning occurs and produces unexpected communities that are ready to respond to the wasting of lives and livelihoods. This part of the COVID-19 pandemic has been less reported and studied, but in several countries people have started to self-organize, building an infrastructure of solidarity and support, focused specifically on helping the most vulnerable in the community. In several countries, People's Solidarity Brigades have been created with precisely this aim in mind. On their website, the People's Solidarity Brigades present themselves as a "network of self-initiated mutual aid groups acting for self-defense by the people for the people."[22] In times of crisis, solidarity is not uncommon; in the current pandemic charity organizations have also mobilized to support those who were most hit by the economic consequences of the virus. Without any intention to diminish the generous effort made by those organizations, in this section I will focus instead on the most politicized of those groups, since I believe that their approach to the pandemic more openly presents a challenge for the Wasteocene regime. As Lauren T. Hudson (2020, 175–176)) has written, charity might reproduce class divisions, while mutual aid aims "to change relationships between people . . . as an act of solidarity and of commitment to interdependence".

For instance, on the Solidarity Brigades' website there is a clear attack against the current economic system which they consider responsible for the crisis:

> We are well aware that governments are no solution to the health crisis. They serve a system based on profit and private interest which is at the root of the current social disaster and of the catastrophic situation public health services find themselves in. . . . This network of solidarity must also focus on denouncing neoliberal policies. They have demonstrated once again their criminal nature. We must elaborate new forms of collective organisation.

Naomi Klein (2008) has theorized the disaster capitalism logic as a mechanism which produces profit from extreme crises while experimenting with advanced forms of repression and securitization. More recently, various scholars and intellectuals have started to speak of disaster communism as the other side of what extreme events may trigger in society. The US writer Rebecca Solnit has provided a rich gallery of histories of solidarity in times of disasters; as she writes:

---

[22] www.brigades.info.

> The history of disaster demonstrates that most of us are social animals,
> hungry for connection, as well as for purpose and meaning. It also suggests
> that if this is who we are, then everyday life in most places is a disaster that
> disruptions sometimes give us a chance to change. (Solnit 2009, 305)

In his book *Extreme Cities,* Ashley Dawson argues that the grassroots self-
organized responses to major disasters should be understood as experiments in
disaster communism. In the momentary disruption of what I have called the
Wasteocene order, new possibilities become feasible; commoning practices
clash with the usual wasting relationships, subverting the usual worth vs
disposable logic. As Dawson writes:

> Capitalism no longer seems the only possible future. We may even begin to
> enact a different society based on human empathy and mutual aid. Communal
> solidarities forged in the teeth of calamity can be seen as a form of disaster
> communism, under which people begin to organize themselves to meet one
> another's basic needs and to collectively survive. (Dawson 2017, 132)

In several Italian cities, the Brigate di Solidarietà Attiva [proactive solidarity
brigades] were created as early as March 2020. Generally, the network over-
lapped with preexisting grassroots organizations, mostly with the centri
sociali,[23] which constituted the logistic infrastructure of this initiative; but it
is also true that this experience went far beyond the centri sociali, involving
a wider number of volunteers. The geography of the pandemic has also influenced the distribution of the solidarity brigades, with a strong presence in the
area of Milan. In an online interview, one activist from Milan speaks of four
hundred volunteers, organized in twelve brigades with a common coordination
committee (Adil 2020). The brigades have provided basic necessities, chiefly
creating food banks and a capillary distribution of food. Sometimes, in the bags
packed with pasta and canned tomatoes, people have also found books, flyers on
the Care Income Campaign, or questionnaires regarding their needs. Often
those brigades have been named after Italian partisans who have fought against
the Nazi-Fascist regime. While distributing food or medicine, the brigades have
also contributed in building alternative narratives, recovering stories of resistance from the memory dumps I have described in section 3.1. In their documents and interviews, all the activists have stressed the continuity between the
COVID-19 crisis and the pre-pandemic "normality." A young activist of the
brigade named after Arcide Cristei – a young partisan killed by the fascists –
argues that the virus has only revealed and exacerbated the injustices already
present in Italian society; for her, the slogan "the normality was the problem" is

---

[23] The Centri Sociali (Social Centers) are old, abandoned buildings occupied by young activists and
transformed into centers for political, cultural, and recreational activities.

the best way to synthesize the vision of the group (Comito 2020). An activist from another brigade describes Milan as a city deeply segregated between the rich and the poor, connecting the effects of the pandemic to this unjust structure embedded into the urban fabric (Adil 2020). Similarly, for the Sant'Ermete committee in Pisa – a grassroots organization based in a working-class neighborhood – the pandemic has sharpened the ongoing inequalities, but it has not created them (Radio Onda D'Urto 2020). This line of reasoning goes hand in hand with my understanding of the Wasteocene as a regime of normality and not of exception.

Yet stressing the continuity of structural inequalities, the solidarity brigades also make another crucial point: as injustice is structural and not contingent, so is the struggle against it. Within the fractures of the Wasteocene regime, subaltern people have gotten organized, sometimes openly clashing with the forces of wasting reproduction, more often struggling to substitute wasting relationships with commoning. This is radically true for the solidarity brigades in Italy. Rising from the experience of the centri sociali, the brigades are deeply immersed in the culture and practice of commoning; after all, what are the Italian centri sociali if not the concrete utopia of asserting the primacy of the commons against private property? Historically, the centri sociali are often abandoned buildings, privately or publicly owned, which activists have reclaimed for political, social, and cultural activities. In the urban fabric, those centers are often located in marginal areas – where the real estate value is lower –, thereby, embodying the commoning vs wasting conflict. As Massimo De Angelis and Silvia Federici have taught us, commons are not only places owned and used following a logic which is alternative to the private property regime; rather, commons are a set of relationships which are generated by and generative of commons (Garcia Lamarca 2014). Commoning practices are much stronger and abiding than any squatted building. One of the pillars of the Wasteocene regime is that each individual is responsible for herself, a message which becomes even louder in times of crisis. Toxic narratives, as I have illustrated in section 3, blame individuals for being poor, subaltern, or sick. Although implementing some measures for supporting the most vulnerable, the basic message of the authorities – and a plethora of famous people – was precisely that: stay at home, assuming that everybody has a comfortable and safe home, and enough resources to survive. Without even mentioning that for many people, especially women, home is not necessarily the ideal refuge from violence. Commoning practices sabotage the Wasteocene logic because they reproduce social values through inclusion and community building while the latter reproduces inequalities through othering and wasting. More than the distribution of food, the solidarity brigades have contributed to prefigurative politics, which, using the words of one activist from the Ho Chi Minh Brigade in Milan, aim to build autonomous communities, self-organized and in charge of the decisions regarding their territories (she calls this community's decision-making). In her interview, Sofia Blu recounts an interesting story about what happened after the lockdown in the working class neighborhood where her brigade operates:

> The first thing was a massive police operation to vacate an illegally occupied building. People thought that those were not regular tenants, many were Roma. There is indeed an issue with the diverse ethnic groups. (Sofia Blu 2020)

The Wasteocene logic immediately reacted to the kind of political imaginaries mobilized by the solidarity brigades; wasting relationships are powerful especially when they convince subaltern people that someone else is the other, while they can consider themselves on the safe side of the Wasteocene line. Indeed, wasting relationships vs commoning, everywhere.

5.2 The Dump's Flowers

A mafia affiliate from Naples, Italy, has become quite famous for saying on the telephone, while being tapped by the police, that "garbage is gold." He was referring to the immense profitability of toxic waste trafficking, a business that has acquired great significance in the criminal portfolio of the camorra, the Neapolitan mafia.[24] Dumping toxic waste without any precaution can ensure high profits for the criminal organizations and important savings for entrepreneurs with no scruples. Evidently, not only criminal organizations look at waste as a source of profit since the recycling industries has become an important, profitable sector worldwide. This does not question, but rather, confirm the general assumption of this Element: capitalism makes profit out of waste. In this section I will not deal with the economics of waste recycling and the possibilities to use it for making profits. Perhaps no one better than Martin Medina (2007) has contributed to a more balanced appraisal of the world of waste pickers, uncovering even the positive sides of the occupation. Making a living extracting resources from the open veins of waste flows is not per se an act of resistance or sabotage against the Wasteocene. But it might become – or be narrated – as such, when it enhances the creation of resisting communities which fight back against the Wasteocene logic. In this sense, I prefer to speak of flowers rather than gold from dumps, to convey the possibility of generating

---

[24] On organized crimes and waste see Lukas 2012. For an ecocritical approach to this theme see Past 2013.

positive, resistant, and empowering communities from the extreme frontiers of the Wasteocene.

The movie *Waste Land* (Walker et al. 2010) documents the two-year project of the Brazilian artist Vik Muniz in the gigantic landfill Jardim Gramacho, in Rio de Janeiro, working with the local waste pickers association. Despite all the complications of this case, brightly illustrated by Kathleen M. Millar (2018) and the limits of Muniz's project (Kantaris 2016), nonetheless, I am employing it because it evokes a wider tradition of grassroots organizations of waste pickers who have fought to achieve recognition and dignity beyond better working conditions. For Melanie Samson (2009), waste pickers' "ontological insurrection" aiming for dignity is foundational for any struggle to improve their material conditions. In presenting his project, Muniz describes the dump as

> the place where everything which is not good goes, including people. The people I will work with in Brazilian society are not different from garbage. (Walker et al. 2010)

Later on in the documentary, several waste pickers confirm this argument. Isis, a young woman working at the dump, declares that she feels dirty. Magna explains how on the bus on her way back home, everybody looks at her with disdain, because her smell clearly reveals who she is. When Muniz and his crew begin to film at the Jardim Gramacho someone asks, jokingly, whether they were making some animal documentary. I interpret this as an ironic denunciation of the invisibility of waste pickers in the global media, where wild animals are indeed much more present. However, I would argue that no matter how much present they might be in the mainstream media, yet wild animals are also oppressed by the Wasteocene logic which either destroys their habitats or transforms them into marketable goods. Again, any true liberation from the Wasteocene cannot be anything but multispecies.

Muniz's project is a beautiful act of resistance against the Wasteocene; the artist, who grew up in a working-class Brazilian family, included a group of catadores – waste pickers – in producing a series of amazing pieces of art using the garbage from the landfill. As the Wasteocene imposes that these people are garbage, Muniz's project appropriates this assumption and overturns it. The powerful portraits of those catadores are made of recycled materials but they are not garbage at all; actually, one of them was sold in an auction in London, while altogether they became an extremely successful exhibition at the Museum of Modern Art in Rio. The selling of the portraits and the prizes received for the movie helped the association of waste pickers to realize some of their objectives, including the acquisition of some trucks and the creation of a public library in the favela. However, more than for the material support for the catadores,

I believe that Muniz's project was successful in challenging the main pillar of the Wasteocene, that is, the othering regime which produces worthless people who not only work with waste but are deemed waste themselves. Looking at the intersection of race and waste, Charles Mills has unequivocally stated that "black has already the connotation of trashiness" (2001, 84). Recognition is an important part of Muniz's project; the waste pickers are not an object of the artist's gaze but they are artists themselves. The exhibition at the Modern Art Museum in Rio de Janeiro is an occupation of the cultural space of the city; for the catadores it was the first time they set foot in a museum and they did so through both their portraits and their bodies.

While Muniz's project is a powerful challenge to the Wasteocene logic, it is equally crucial to recognize that his work intertwined with the existing social organization among the waste pickers. The catadores working with the artist were all members of the Associação dos Catadores do Aterro Metropolitano de Jardim Gramacho, and the fact that they were organized was in itself an important piece in their strategy to fight back the Wasteocene logic of disposability. Several of the waste pickers express their sense of pride in being part of an organization which, evidently, gives them identity and purpose that the wasting relationships strive to erase. Valter, one of the older members of the association, expresses beautifully the work done by the organization well beyond the mere planning of the recycling. Valter supports Munitz's project on the basis that it will help to enhance the "recognition of the catadores as a class," in line with the approach of the Brazilian association of waste pickers (Movimento Nacional dos Catadores de Materiais Recicláveis) (Samson 2009, 42). Introducing himself, Valter explains that he did not have any formal education but he is proud to represent 2500 waste pickers working in the landfill. The politicization of this work slips at a certain point from his lips, when, apparently out of context, Valter tells some fellow waste pickers: "The fight is long, comrades, but victory is certain." At the end of the movie, we discover that Valter died of lung cancer just after having met Vik Munitz. We know too little about him, but his story is as a telling example of the contradictions of surviving within and against the Wasteocene. New identities and pride can come from social struggles but this should not make us undervalue the power of the Wasteocene regime which in the end can invade our cells and our bodies. If this means that the Wasteocene has won, I would not be so sure about it.

5.3 Dancing around the (Toxic) Fire

"Everything changes when we look at it from the barricades" – my dear friend Damir Arsenijevic was repeating this almost like a mantra, during his time as a visiting scholar at the Environmental Humanities Laboratory in Stockholm. His work in Tuzla, Bosnia-Herzegovina, on toxicity, war, and workers' struggles resonates intimately with my own research on the Wasteocene. In a powerful piece, entitled the *Proletarian Lung* Damir Arsenijevic writes:

> The disruption between monetized death and 'grievable life' means to start from that which is 'ungrievable' life in Bosnia and Herzegovina today. I must start with the "proletarian lung" of the metal picker whose lungs get burned by the left-over chlorine in HAK [Chlorine Alkaline Power House] pipes, who succumbs to his injuries and dies. His death is the toll of the extractive logic of predatory capitalism in Bosnia & Herzegovina today. (Arsenijevic 2019)

Indeed, the former industrial city of Tuzla could have easily been a telling vignette in my subsection 3.3 on the Wasteocene local and global, alongside Cancer Alley in Louisiana and Rio Doce in Brazil. As Arsenijevic has explained to me, in Tuzla the toxic legacy of the war merges with the toxic legacy of industrial pollution under ethnocapitalism and privatization; a toxicity literally buried in the landscape and in the bodies of Bosnians. The entire country of Bosnia-Herzegovina seems to be a living proof of what wasting relationships can produce at their extreme.

Nevertheless, Tuzla is not only another point on the map of the Wasteocene. It is also the vibrant ground of resistance and prefigurative politics. The barricades evoked by Damir are not a metaphor, a rhetorical figure for a radical piece of scholarship; they were made of wood and scrap metal, of bodies and tents, fires and banners, and they served to protect the DITA factory – a chemical plant – from their owners and the risk to be dismantled and sold out, piece after piece, as many other factories had been in the area. Nothing particularly original, after all: everywhere, global capitalism acts as a parasite, invading the productive tissues of communities, squeezing the most out of them, and fleeing as soon as the margins for profit become too small, but not without leaving a long lasting legacy of toxicity. Worthless people, worthless communities, worthless states – this is how Wasteocene history and geography become embedded within the Balkans. The barricades were the material demonstration that subaltern people, and first of all the workers, did not accept quietly to be wasted. Evidently, those workers and their allies were defending their jobs and incomes, but in doing so, they were also building a wider social movement, reclaiming the commons against privatization and individualization brought by the neoliberal agenda. In February 2014 the entire Bosnia-Herzegovina was traversed by a massive uprising, a truly grassroots movement with both a specific set of requests and a wider political agenda. The creation of the plenums – citizens' assemblies – was the most innovative and generative social innovation produced during the uprising. In Tuzla, the institution of the plenum was deeply affected by a positive dialectic with the local university, which brought the creation of the Workers' University.[25] As with the associations of waste pickers, also in the case of the Workers' University, the scope of the resistant practices generated in the struggles went far beyond the specific demands about working conditions or cleanup operations. With Hardt and Negri (2017), I argue that those assemblies should be seen as an experimentation of those "independent institutions" through which new democratic political possibilities are opened (xx-xxi).

As Arsenijevic writes, the plenums

> are open, direct, and transparent democracy in practice. The Plenum, as the form of self-organization and the method of work, in which citizens come together to articulate demands, is underpinned by the action of the protests. (Arsenijevic 2014, 48)

While fighting for jobs and for the cleaning up of former industrial areas, those activists were actually reclaiming the commons in the widest sense possible, that is, as an alternative organization of social life, a defense of the health of people and places, and a counter-hegemonic storytelling of their collective past. As a matter of fact, the Workers' University has a strong commitment to the creation and preservation of a collective memory as proved by its involvement in a graphic novel project about the movement (Šehabović, Gaknič and Arsenijevic 2020), the creation of a multimedia archive, and the rediscovery of past histories of rebellion, such as Husino workers' general strikes from the 1920s for better conditions of life and work (Husarić 2014, 70).

Memories and recognition are also at the core of another struggle which dances around the metaphorical toxic fire of a dismissed industrial complex in Rome, Italy. I have discovered the story of the SNIA Viscosa factory through the music video of the Italian hip hop artist, Assalti frontali (2014). The music video, beautifully entitled *Il lago che combatte* [The resisting lake], tells the story of how the rise of a lake in the middle of a dismissed industrial area stopped a development plan aiming to transform that complex in a shopping mall/residential area.

> Within the cement monsters/This body of water reflects the sky/It is nature fighting back/This neighborhood is less dark now! (Assalti frontali 2016)

---

[25] In their website, the Workers' university is defined as "an initiative that ensures the active participation of citizens in the economic and political life of BiH with an emphasis on issues of public good." http://radnickiuniverzitet.org/o-radnickom-univerzitetu

Feminist environmental humanities scholar Mirian Tola has brilliantly explored the case of the SNIA Viscosa factory and its postindustrial lake. The factory worked from 1923 to 1954, producing a synthetic fiber – rayon – through the use of carbon disulfide, an extremely toxic chemical substance. The Wasteocene logic of wasting and othering applied to both the workers, who were exposed to the harmful effects of the carbon disulfide, and the entire human and more-than human community, which was also affected by the diffuse toxicity. As Mirian Tola has written:

> Workers, water, trees, and other raw materials were vital resources in the viscose productive process. The chemical violence welded to the rayon industry reduced workers to a kind of waste that was discarded and moved from one enclosed space to another, from the factory to the hospital. (Tola 2019, 203)

After the interruption of the production, the factory was abandoned for decades up to the 1990s and 2000s when it became the target of several development projects aiming to transform the industrial area in a shopping mall or a residential complex. While a grassroots movement began to mobilize to defend the area, occupying part of the buildings for cultural and political activities, even nature seemed to fight back against the development project. The factory had been built in a marshy area, precisely to take advantage of the abundance of water, but when the new development project started, the same water reemerged from the ground, creating a large lake in the middle of the former industrial setting. The developers tried to stop the formation of the lake, pumping water into the sewage system, yet this only resulted in the gigantic overflooding of the entire neighborhood. In the end, the lake stabilized itself by beckoning birds, humans and other animals in a sort of multispecies alliance which succeeded in stopping the development project. Upon the ruins of an industrial toxic past, a commoning experience was born; one which led to the creation of a natural park and a social center, both self-managed by grassroots activists. The SNIA Viscosa story sheds light on the Wasteocene logic and the possible alternatives to it. Recovering what has been wasted, that is, putting it again at work, is a possible outcome of the Wasteocene logic. A shopping mall can sprout from the ruins of an abandoned factory, but this does not question at all the wasting relationships which have contaminated workers and their community. What radically challenges the Wasteocene logic is commoning as a practice, because it creates a different set of relationships based on reproduction and recognition rather than exploitation and obliteration. For this reason, both Tola and the activists stress the link between the struggle for the park and the cultivation and preservation of workers' memories of toxic oppression and social mobilization. As the Wasteocene manifests itself through the imposition of toxic narratives and the erasure of the stories of resistance, so the struggle against it also passes through the construction of alternative archives as those created by the Workers' University in Tuzla and by the Ex SNIA activists in Rome, who have found and recovered the files of the workers. Tellingly, the SNIA historical archive has been named after Maria Baccante, a factory worker who had fought as a partisan against the Nazi-Fascist regime, later becoming a leader of the 1949 massive protest against layoffs in the factory. Together with the stories of the workers, the activists have also recovered the stories of the nonhuman presence in the area, tracking the fascinating histories of the underground water or learning about the birds and plants which have come back to the area. To fight back against the Wasteocene logic the activists need to build new relationships amongst themselves and with the environment, because the park they created was not only the preservation of a "natural area" but the reinvention of a multispecies community based on commoning practices rather than on exploitation and othering.

Sometimes, indeed, people can dance around a toxic fire in the sense that they might find the reasons and strength to imagine and practice new communities by building upon their experiences of being wasted. Damir Arsenijevic writes that one of the participants of the plenum in Tuzla said that for him being part of the protests was like being on a holiday, meaning with it the happiness and the breaking of the normal he felt through that experience. Similarly, the SNIA activists have enjoyed the opportunity brought by the wasted landscapes and toxic stories from the factory to create a lively and welcoming environment in the middle of a working-class neighborhood. Sergio Ruiz Cayuela (2018) has recovered a similar story from Catalonia. There, a subaltern community has been able to reinvent itself through the struggles for better conditions of life. Also in the story of Can Sant Joan town, the presence of a highly polluting factory has catalyzed the mobilization of citizens fighting back against the Wasteocene logic. While wasting relationships made this community an ideal location for several unwanted infrastructures and productions, including a cement plant, the local inhabitants have strived to build a different set of socio-ecological relationships. In the interviews published by Sergio Ruiz Cayuela, the toxicity of the factory emerges through two different paths: on the one hand, the dust entering everywhere, in the homes and in the lungs of people, on the other hand, the money through which the factory aims to buy everything and everyone in the community. In this sense, the struggle of the neighborhood association can be truly considered a liberation struggle, aiming to reverse the wasting relationships which make profit on the devaluation of life. Again, in Can Sant Joan, as in Tuzla or in Rome, reclaiming the memories of past struggles is as crucial as mobilizing in the present.[26] Several activists spoke of their town as a rebel community with a long history of social mobilization. The fight to stop the pollution coming from the factory has had several collateral advantages for the community, such as the creation of a social center, the development of cultural projects, including poetry readings and film forums, a community newspaper, and the participation in national and international activists' networks. Describing one of the cultural campaigns of the neighborhood association, Antonio Alcántara, one of the interviewees, states

> It brings us together, it transforms us, it allows us to generate or to build different relationships. Through the cultural factor you can build alternatives to the existing status quo. (Ruiz Cayuela 2018, 40)

The dust is still in the air, the chimneys dominate the skyline of the town, the smell can be revolting, but the community is not anymore on the paycheck of the factory; that is not a wasted community.[27] People are dancing around that toxic fire. As if it was a holiday.

6 Conclusion

I am finalizing this manuscript in the midst of the COVID-19 pandemic, while more than 20 million people have been infected and 700 thousand have died, worldwide. This situation would have affected my writing anyway, but it did hit me in an extreme way since I was infected by the virus in the early March 2020. Besides slowing down drastically the completion of this manuscript, my COVID-19 experience has also brought other things into this project. In section 5 I decided to include the experience of the solidarity brigades, which have been created to support people economically affected by the virus, as an example of the struggles within and against the Wasteocene. This implies that I interpret COVID-19 as one example of what I have called "epiphanies" of the Wasteocene, that is, those revelatory moments which open a fracture in the normalizing structure of the Wasteocene, exposing the other side of the wasting line. Arundhati Roy has defined the current pandemic as a "portal, a gateway between one world and the next" (Roy 2020) and several communities on the ground are trying to keep that portal open toward a more just and progressive future.

Indeed, the fact that I have been severely ill with the virus does not mean that the ordering principle of the Wasteocene has been radically twisted. My COVID-19 experience speaks more of my privileges rather than of the equalizer

---

[26] Pasquale Verdicchio (2016, 141) speaks of a narrative rehabilitation of contaminated places.

[27] For a similar process of resignification of landscape and memories in the Campania region, see De Rosa 2018.

power of the virus. Paraphrasing Rob Nixon (2019), we may all be in this pandemic, but not under the same conditions. As with every epiphany, also with COVID-19 has the Wasteocene logic become more evident precisely when the solid wall between those who are deemed valuable and the disposable others start showing some breaches. Many sources are pointing to the unequal distribution of the virus, and especially of the death tolls, in a tragic reproduction of wasted lives and places. When implemented, the quarantine has brought unequal effects on different segments of the population, hitting the most vulnerable the hardest. But as I have shown in section 5.2, COVID-19 has also generated prefigurative grassroots experiences, which have fought to knock down the Wasteocene logic rather than restore it. The breaches in the wall should not be repaired, they should instead offer leverage to tear down the entire wall.

In the end, I wonder what would make this Element a success. Naturally, I would be glad if I manage to persuade the reader that the Wasteocene is a useful concept in order to understand the socio-ecological crisis. Exercising the eye to see the wasting relationships which produce wasted people and places would also be a remarkable result. As I have repeated throughout this text, invisibilization and normalization are two pillars of the Wasteocene logic which not only wastes people and ecosystems but also imposes toxic narratives while either obliterating or domesticating any alternative stories. For this reason, the struggles against the Wasteocene are always struggles over contested memories, recovering counter-hegemonic narratives which build alternative identities. As the Wasteocene regime aims to produce disposable people and places, dismantling it needs more than technical solutions for managing waste or toxicity. Wasting relationships must be substituted with new socio-ecological relationships, which are not designed in a laboratory or prescribed in academic volumes, but alive and experimented everywhere within the very fractures of the Wasteocene. In the previous sections, I offered some glimpses of these experiments, arguing that at their very core they have always been rooted in commoning practices. As wasting relationships are based on appropriation and exclusion so commoning practices are made of sharing and caring.

These are the main ideas presented in this Element through what I hope was a fruitful combination of theoretical arguments and empirical cases. If some of these ideas have sparked the curiosity of the reader, I assume it was a success. Someone else will measure the success of this volume with bibliometric parameters, counting how many quotations it will gain. A few colleagues told me that I might get lucky because I invented "my own word," something which apparently can be a cure-all remedy in the Publish-or-Perish winter in which our academic system has ended up. But the Wasteocene is nothing radically new.

I am not claiming to have found a new geological era; I have neither the expertise nor the ambition to find the golden spike of the Wasteocene. Is the Wasteocene a concept radically independent from those of necro/racial capitalism, coloniality, and environmental justice? No, it is not. Those concepts are deeply and organically related. I refuse the neoliberal credo that implies the creative wasting of something/someone in order to claim to be anew.

While acknowledging my intellectual debt and linkages with a larger radical tradition, I do believe that mobilizing the concept of the Wasteocene can help us to understand some crucial features of the current socio-ecological crisis. It reminds us that exploitation and oppression are always embedded within the bodies of humans and nonhumans. It tells us that for a radical emancipatory project taking control of the means of production is not enough unless we do not change the socio-ecological relationships from wasting to commoning. The Wasteocene offers a narrative which binds together humans and nonhumans through wasting relationships, neither equating them nor renouncing to name the culprits (that is, accepting the Anthropocene formula saying that "all humans are responsible"). Finally, at least for some scholars, the Wasteocene might offer an interpretative tool which can also be employed beyond the borders of what is recognized as "capitalism" (although, I would argue that capitalism has many faces . . .).

My reflections on the Wasteocene are generated in a fruitful intellectual exchange with many scholars and activists. My debt to the StopBiocidio activists in Naples is immense; it is with them that I have experienced what it means to live on the other side of the Wasteocene divide and politicize your own body to fight against wasting relationships and toxic narratives. The concept of the Capitalocene, with its multiple, rhizomatic origins, is foundational to my own reflection, because it clarifies that it is not a generic human subject but a way of organizing production and society that has brought the socio-ecological crisis. Other scholars have shed light on the colonial roots of the Anthropocene and its othering project; I have been deeply influenced by Heather Davis and Zoe Todd, Kyle P. Whyte, Andrew Baldwin and Bruce Erickson. Through Laura Pulido I have learned of the intrinsic connections of capitalism and racism (and of Cedric Robinson's work). David Pellow, Julie Sze, and Robert Bullard have taught me that some communities have been created for the sole purpose of becoming the socio-ecological dumps of someone else's well-being. Joan Martinez Alier has provided the most comprehensive database of ecological conflicts, or, as I would call it, the most rich atlas of the Wasteocene. Without Stacy Alaimo I would have not been able to understand the embodiment of toxicity, while both Alaimo and Serenella Iovino have initiated me to the liberation power of narratives. Rob Nixon opened my eyes on the different temporalities of environmental violence; without slow violence, I would have not been able to see the long lasting unfolding of the Wasteocene. This Element comes after Stefania Barca's meticulous disassembling of what she has called the Anthropocene master's narrative, pointing already to some of the themes I have also developed in my own writing, such as the performative nature of mainstream narratives in oppressing the subalterns and limiting the political imagination. Gregg Mitman and Chris Sellers put the body into the realm of environmental history without forgetting that both bodies and environments are not actors in a neutral network of relations but pieces ordered by power relationships. I first started to think about the Wasteocene in an article I published with Massimo De Angelis and I am in debt to him for my understanding of commoning as a set of practices based on reproduction of both relationships and life. Many of the examples presented in this Element come from the work of friends and former students, such as Damir Arsenijevic, Sergio Ruiz Cayuela, Ilenia Iengo, Giuseppe Orlandini, Miriam Tola, and Daniele Valisena.

Now, can I really claim that the Wasteocene is my own, original, self-created, idea? I can happily think not. It is always commoning vs. appropriation, starting from where one stands. Even from here

References

Adil (2020). Solidarietà ai tempi della pandemia, 4 May 2020, podcast, www
.spreaker.com/show/la-stanza-di-adil.

Afan de Rivera, C. (1825). *Memoria intorno alle devastazioni prodotte dalle
acque a cagion de' diboscamenti*, Napoli: Reale Tipografia della guerra.

Agamben, G. (2010). *The State of Exception*, Chicago: Chicago University
Press.

Alaimo, S. (2010). *Bodily Natures: Science, Environment, and the Material
Self*, Bloomington: Indiana University Press.

Allen, B. (2003). *Uneasy Alchemy. Citizens and Experts in Louisiana's
Chemical Corridor Disputes*, Cambridge (MA): MIT Press.

Angela Rosa (2017). Fighting oil and natural gas exploration. www.toxicbios
.eu/#/stories.

Angus, I. (2016). *Facing the Anthropocene. Fossil Capitalism and the Crisis of
the Earth System*, New York: Monthly Review Press.

Armiero, M. (2011). *A Rugged Nation. Mountains and the Making of Modern
Italy*, Cambridge (UK): White Horse Press.

Armiero, M., & D'Alisa, G. (2012). Rights of resistance: the garbage struggles
for environmental justice in Campania, Italy. *Capitalism Nature Socialism*,
23(4), 52–68. http://doi.org/10.1080/10455752.2012.724200.

Armiero, M. & Fava, A. (2016). Of humans, sheep, and dioxin: A history of
contamination and transformation in Acerra, Italy. *Capitalism Nature
Socialism*, **27**(2), 67–82. http://doi.org/10.1080/10455752.2016.1172812.

Armiero, M. & De Rosa, S. P. (2016). Political Effluvia: Smells, Revelations, and the
Politicization of Daily Experience in Naples, Italy. In J. Thorpe, S. Rutherford,
L. A. Sandberg, eds., *Methodological Challenges in Nature-Culture and
Environmental History Research*, London: Routledge, pp. pp.173–186.

Armiero, M. & De Angelis, M. (2017). Anthropocene: Victims, narrators, and
revolutionaries. *South Atlantic Quarterly*, **116**(2), 345–362. http://doi.org/
10.1215/00382876-3829445.

Armiero, M. (2019). Sabotaging the Anthropocene. Or, in Praise of Mutiny. In
G. Mitman, M. Armiero and R. S. Emmett, eds., *Future Remains. A Cabinet
of Curiosities for the Anthropocene*, Chicago: Chicago University Press, pp.
129–139.

Arsenijevic, D. (2014). Protests and Plenums. The Struggle for the Commons.
In D. Arsenijevic, ed., *Unbribable Bosnia and Herzegovina*, Baden-Baden:
Nomos, pp. 45–50.

Arsenijevic, D. (2019). The proletarian lung. The struggle for the commons as memory politics in Bosnia and Herzegovina. *Springerin* 1 www.springerin .at/en/2019/1/die-proletarische-lunge/.

Assalti frontali (2016). Il lago che combatte. In *Mille gruppi avanzano* music album.

Baczynska, G. (2013). Putin accused of Soviet tactics in drafting new history book, 18 November 2013 www.reuters.com/article/us-russia-history/putin-accused-of-soviet-tactics-in-drafting-new-history-book-idUSBRE9AH0JK20131118.

Baine, W. B., Mazzotti, M., Greco, D., et al. (1974). Epidemiology of Cholera in Italy in 1973. *The Lancet*, **304**(7893), 1370–1374.

Barca, S. (2020). *Forces of Reproduction. Notes for a Counter-Hegemonic Anthropocene*, Cambridge (MA): Cambridge University Press.

Bauman, Z. (2004). *Wasted Lives. Modernity and its Outcasts*, Cambridge (UK): Polity.

Bauman, Z. (2007). *Consuming Life*, Cambridge (UK): Polity.

Baurick, T. & Meiners, J. (2019). Welcome to "Cancer Alley," where toxic air is about to get worse, Oct. 30, 2019, available online at www.propublica .org/article/welcome-to-cancer-alley-where-toxic-air-is-about-to-get-worse.

BBC (2019). Brazil textbooks 'to be revised to deny 1964 coup, 4 April 2019, www.bbc.com/news/world-latin-america-47813480.

Berruti, G. & Palestino, M.F. (2020) Contested land and blurred rights in the Land of Fires (Italy). *International Planning Studies*, **25**(3), 277–288. http:// doi.org/10.1080/13563475.2019.1584551.

Biehler, D. (2013). *Pests in the City: Flies, Bedbugs, Cockroaches, and Rats*, Seattle: University of Washington Press.

Blacksmith Institute (2013). *The worlds worst. 2013: The top ten toxic threats*, New York, www.worstpolluted.org/docs/TopTenThreats2013.pdf.

Bollier D. & Helfrich, S. (2012). *The Wealth of the Commons: A World Beyond Market and State*, Amherst (MA): Levellers Press.

Bonneuil, C. & Fressoz, J.-B. (2017). *The Shock of the Anthropocene. The Earth, History and Us*, London: Verso.

Borowy, I. (2019). Hazardous waste: The beginning of international organizations addressing a growing global challenge in the 1970s. *Worldwide Waste: Journal of Interdisciplinary Studies*, **2**(1), 1–10. http://doi.org/ 10.5334/wwwj.39.

Cave, P. (2013). Japanese colonialism and the Asia-Pacific War in Japan's history textbooks: Changing representations and their causes. *Modern Asian Studies*, **47**(2): 542–580. http://doi.org/10.1017/S0026749X11000485.

Cayuela Ruiz, S. (2018). *Rejecting fate. The challenge of a subaltern community to the creation of a sacrifice zone in Can Sant Joan, Catalonia* (Master Thesis), KTH Royal Institute of Technology, Stockholm. urn: nbn:se:kth: diva-225837.

Chakrabarty, D. (2009). The climate of history: four theses. *Critical Inquiry*, **35** (2), 197–222.

Chakrabarty, D. (1992). Of garbage, modernity and the citizen's gaze. *Economic and Political Weekly*, **27**(10/11), 541–547.

Chubb, J. (1980). Naples under the Left: The limits of local change. *Comparative Politics*, **13**(1), 53–78. http://doi.org/10.2307/421763.

Ciccone, A. (2010). Nell'inferno di Terzigno, *L'Espresso* 11 October 2010, available at https://espresso.repubblica.it/attualita/cronaca/2010/10/11/news/ nell-inferno-di-terzigno-1.24800.

Comito, A. (2020). COVID 19 storie di solidarietà, Reportage, video available at www.youtube.com/watch?v=yxEQSEQbkF4.

Coordinamento provinciale salute FLM, Medicina democratica, Magistratura democratica (1979). *Libro bianco sulle origini, ragioni, responsabilità del "male oscuro", Prospettive assistenziali*, n. 46, aprile – giugno 1979 availabe at www.fondazionepromozionesociale.it/PA_Indice/046/46_napoli_libro_ bianco_sulle_origini.htm

Corbin, A. (1986). *The Foul and the Fragrant: Odor and the French Social Imagination,* Leamington Spa (UK): Berg Publishers Lt [French ed. 1982].

Corongiu, M. (2017). Agriculture against the Land of Fires, www.toxicbios.eu/ #/stories.

Costa, N., director (n. d.). *Rio Doce Rio Morto*, documentário para Canal Drauzio Varella, https://drauziovarella.uol.com.br/videos/especiais/rio-doce-rio-morto/.

Crescenti, U. (2009). Relazione di consulenza tecnica nell'indagine ambientale sulla discarica Difrabi presso Pianura, in provincia di Napoli, Chieti 5 June 2009, Procura della Repubblica presso il tribunale di Napoli, vi sezione, procedimento penale n. 1499/08 RGNR, 6.

Crutzen, P., & Stoermer, E. F. (2000). The "Anthropocene." *IGBP newsletter*, **4**(1), 17–18.

D'Alisa, G., Burgalassi, D., Healy, H., and Walter, M., (2010). Conflict in Campania: waste emergency or crisis of democracy? *Ecological Economics*, **70**(2), 239–249. http://doi.org/10.1016/j.ecolecon.2010.06.021.

Davies, T. (2018). Toxic space and time: slow violence, necropolitics, and petrochemical pollution. *Annals of the American Association of Geographers*, **108**(6), 1537–1553. http://doi.org/10.1080/24694452.2018.1470924.

Davis, J. Moulton, A., Van Sant, L., Williamset, B. (2019). Anthropocene, Capitalocene, … Plantationocene? A Manifesto for ecological justice in an age of global crises. *Geography Compass*, **13**(5), e12438. http://doi.org/10.1111/gec3.12438.

Dawson, A. (2017). *Extreme Cities*, London: Verso.

De Angelis, M. (2007). *The Beginning of History. Value Struggles and Global Capital*, London: Pluto Press.

De Angelis, M. (2017). *Omnia Sunt Communia: On the Commons and the Transformation to Postcapitalism*, London: Zed Books.

De Simone, A., Medolla, W., and Petricciuolo, S. (2011). *Nelle terre di Gomorra*, video reportage in four episodes for Current tv, available at http://youtubedownloaderonline.org/video/0AXeSxC5glU/-Nelle%20Terre%20di%20Gomorra-%20Current%20Tv.html.

Dean, W. (1995). *With Broadax and Firebrand: The Destruction of the Brazilian Atlantic Coastal Forest*, Berkeley: University of California Press.

De Rosa, S.P. (2018). A political geography of 'waste wars' in Campania (Italy): Competing territorialisations and socio-environmental conflicts. *Political Geography*, **67**, 46–55. http://doi.org/0.1016/j.polgeo.2018.09.009.

Di Chiro, G. (2017). Welcome to the White (M)Anthropocene? A Feminist-Environmentalist Critique. In S. Macgregor, ed., *Routledge Handbook of Gender and Environment*, London: Routledge, pp. 487–505.

Ernstson, H. & Swyngedouw, E., eds. (2019). *Urban Political Ecology in the Anthropo-obscene*, London: Routledge.

Erodoto108 (2018). Taranto.2/ Ritorno sopra i Tamburi, www.erodoto108.com/taranto-2ritorno-sopra-i-tamburi/.

Fernandes, G. W., Goulart F.F., Ranieri, B.D., et al. (2016). Deep into the mud: Ecological and socio-economic impacts of the dam breach in Mariana, Brazil. *Natureza & Conservação*, **14**(2), 35–45. http://doi.org/10.1016/j.ncon.2016.10.003.

Fittipaldi, E. (2011). Campania col veleno in corpo, *L'Espresso* **24** March 2011.

Fucini, R. (1878). *Napoli a occhio nudo*, Firenze: Successori Le Monnier.

Galeano, E. (1997). *Open Veins of Latin America. 25th anniversary ed.*, London: Latin America Bureau.

Garcia Lamarca, M. (2014). *Federici and De Angelis on the political ecology of the commons*, 10 August 2014, available at https://undisciplinedenvironments.org/2014/08/10/federici-and-de-angelis-on-the-political-ecology-of-the-commons/.

Gautieri, G. (1815). *Notizie elementari sui nostri boschi,* Napoli: Angelo Trani.

Geremicca, A. (1979). Non è oscuro il male di Napoli, *l'Unità* 24 January 1979 availabe at https://archivio.unita.news/assets/derived/1979/01/24/issue_full.pdf.

Gille, Z. (2007). *From the Cult of Waste to the Trash Heap of History: The Politics of Waste in Socialist and Postsocialist Hungary*, Bloomington: Indiana University Press.

Giuliani, G. (2021). *Monsters, Catastrophes and the Anthropocene: A Postcolonial Critique*, London: Routledge.

Goldstein, D. (2020). Two states. Eight textbooks. Two American stories, *The New York Times* 12 January 2020, www.nytimes.com/interactive/2020/01/12/us/texas-vs-california-history-textbooks.html.

Hamilton, C. (2015). The theodicy of the "Good Anthropocene." *Environmental Humanities*, 7(1), 233–238.

Hamilton, C. (2017). *Defiant Earth: The Fate of Humans in the Anthropocene*, Cambridge (UK): Polity.

Haraway, D. (2015). Anthropocene, Capitalocene, Plantationocene, Chthulucene: making kin. *Environmental Humanities*, 6(1), 159–165. http://doi.org/10.1215/22011919-3615934.

Hardt, M., & Negri, A. (2017). *Assembly*, New York: Oxford University Press.

Hawkins, G. (2006). *The Ethics of Waste: How We Relate to Rubbish*, Oxford (UK): Rowman & Littlefield.

Heacock, M., Kelly, C.B., Asante, K.A. et al. (2016). E-waste and harm to vulnerable populations: A growing global problem. *Environmental Health Perspective*, 124(5), 550–555. http://doi.org/10.1289/ehp.1509699.

Hicks, H. J. (2016). *The Post-Apocalyptic Novel in the Twenty-First Century*, New York: Palgrave Macmillan.

Hornborg, A. (2015). The Political Ecology of the Technocene: Uncovering Ecologically Unequal Exchange in the World-System. In C Hamilton, C Bonneuil, and F Gemenne, eds., *The Anthropocene and the Global Environmental Crisis: Rethinking Modernity in a New Epoch*, London: Routledge, pp. 57–69.

Hudson, L. T. (2020). Building where we are: The solidarity-economy response to crisis pandemic and the crisis of capitalism. A Rethinking Marxism dossier, summer 2020, available at http://rethinkingmarxism.org/Dossier2020/, 172–180.

Husarić, H. (2014). February Awakening: Breaking with the Political Legacy of the Last 20 Years. In D. Arsenijevic, ed., *Unbribable Bosnia and Herzegovina*, Baden-Baden: Nomos, pp. 65–70.

Iovino, S. (2009). Naples 2008, or, the waste land: Trash, citizenship, and an ethic of narration. *Neohelicon*, 36, 335–346. http://doi.org/10.1007/s11059-009-0004-6.

Iovino, S. (2016). *Ecocriticism and Italy. Ecology, Resistance, and Liberation*, London: Bloomsbury Academic.

Iovino, S. (2016). Pollution. In J. Adamson, W. A. Gleason and D. N. Pellow, eds., *Keywords for Environmental Studies*, New York: New York University Press.

Jørgensen, F.A. (2019). *Recycling*, Cambridge (MA): The MIT Press.

Kaika, M. (2017). 'Don't call me resilient again!': the New Urban Agenda as immunology ... or ... what happens when communities refuse to be vaccinated with 'smart cities' and indicators. *Environment & Urbanization*, **29**(1): 89–102. http://doi.org/10.1177/0956247816684763.

Kantaris, G. (2016). Waste Not, Want Not. Garbage and the Philosopher of the Dump (Waste Land and Estamira). In C. Lindner & M. Meissner, eds., *Global Garbage: Urban Imaginaries of Waste, Excess, and Abandonment*, London: Routledge, pp. 52–67.

Kaza, S., Yao, L. Bhada-Tata, P., and Van Woerden, F., (2018). *What a waste 2.0: A global snapshot of solid waste management to 2050*. Washington, DC: World Bank. http://doi.org/10.1596/978–1-4648–1329-0.

Kelley D. G. R. (2000). Foreword. In C. J. Robinson, *Black Marxism: The Making of the Black Radical Tradition*, Chapel Hill: The University of North Carolina Press, 2000 [first ed. 1983 Zed Books].

Kingsley, P. (2018). How Viktor Orban Bends Hungarian Society to His Will, *The New York Times* 27 March 2018, www.nytimes.com/2018/03/27/world/europe/viktor-orban-hungary.html.

Klein N., Whitecross, M., Winterbottom, M. (2009). *Shock Doctrine*, documentary 2009.

Klein, N. (2008). *Shock Doctrine. The Rise of Disaster Capitalism*, London: Penguin Books.

Lambiase, S. & Zappalà, A. (1973). *Napoli al tempo del colera*, documentary Italy 2007.

Landrigan, P. J., Fuller, R., Acosta N.J.R., et al. (2018). Lancet Commission on pollution and health. *The Lancet*, **391**(10119),462–512. http://doi.org/10.1016/S0140-6736(17)32345–0.

Langston, N. (2011). *Toxic Bodies. Hormone Disruptors and the Legacy of DES*, New Haven: Yale University Press.

Lewis, S.L., & Maslin, M. (2018). *The Human Planet: How We Created the Anthropocene*, London: Pelican.

Lombardi, N. (2014). Il mio nome è Nunzia. In M. Armiero, ed., *Teresa e le altre. Storie di donne nella Terra dei Fuochi*, Milano: Jaca Book, pp. 19–41.

Lotta Continua (1973a). Il colera si estende Mercoledì 5 settembre 1973, available at http://fondazionerrideluca.com/web/download/1973/09_1973/LC1_1973_09_5.pdf.

Lotta Continua (1973b). Non solo il colera ha ucciso Francesca Noviello, Domenica 9 settembre, availabe at http://fondazionerrideluca.com/web/download/1973/09_1973/LC1_1973_09_9.pdf.

Lucia (2007). Interview in possession of the author.

Lukas, S. (2012). Crime and Garbage. In C. A. Zimring, ed., *Encyclopedia of Consumption and Waste: The Social Science of Garbage*, London: SAGE publication, pp. 160–163.

Lundgren, K. (2012). *The Global Impact of E-waste: Addressing the Challenge*, Geneva: ILO.

Luppino, F. (2011). Libri di storia: Il Pdl vuole la commissione di inchiesta, *l'Unità* 13 April 2011, http://m.flcgil.it/rassegna-stampa/nazionale/libri-di-storia-il-pdl-vuole-la-commissione-di-inchiesta.flc.

Malm, A. (2020). *Corona, Climate, Chronic Emergency. War Communism in the Twenty-First Century*, London: Verso.

Malm, A., & Hornborg, A. (2014). The geology of mankind? A critique of the Anthropocene narrative. *The Anthropocene Review*, 1(1), 62–69. http://doi.org/10.1177/2053019613516291.

Marco (2011). Interview in possession of the author.

Marques, A. (2017). Arlindo Marques and the Tejo river pollution. www.toxicbios.eu/#/stories.

Marsh, G. P. (1965). *Man and Nature*, edited by D. Lowenthal, Cambridge (MA): Belknap Pr. of Harvard University Press.

McNeill, J. R., & Engelke, P. (2014). *The Great Acceleration: An Environmental History of the Anthropocene since 1945*, Cambridge (MA): Harvard University Press.

Medina, M. (2007). *The World's Scavengers: Salvaging for Sustainable Consumption and Production*, Lanham (MD): AltaMira Press.

Melograni, G. (1810). *Istruzioni fisiche ed economiche dei boschi,* Napoli: Angelo Trani.

Melosi, M. (2005). *Garbage in the City*, Pittsburgh: University of Pittsburgh Press.

Milanez, B. & Losekann, C. eds. (2016). *Desastre no Vale do Rio Doce: Antecedentes, impactos e ações sobre a destruição*, Rio De Janeiro: Folio Digital.

Millar, K. M. (2018). *Reclaiming the Discarded: Life and Labor on Rio's Garbage Dump*, Durham and London: Duke University Press.

Mills, C. (2001). Black Trash. In L. Westra, & B. E. Lawson, eds., *Faces of Environmental Racism*, Lanham: Rowman & Littlefield, pp. 73–91.

Mitman, G. (2019). Hubris or Humility. Genealogies of the Anthropocene. In G. Mitman, M. Armiero and R. S. Emmett, eds., *Future Remains. A Cabinet of Curiosities for the Anthropocene*, Chicago: Chicago University Press, pp. 59–68.

Moore, J., ed. (2016). *Anthropocene or Capitalocene?: Nature, History, and the Crisis of Capitalism*, Oakland (CA): Pm Press.

Musella, A. & Manzo, G. (2012). *Chi comanda Napoli*, Roma, RX.

Nixon, R. (2011). *Slow Violence and the Environmentalism of the Poor*, Cambridge (MA): Harvard University Press.

Nixon, R. (2019). The Anthropocene. The Promise and Pitfalls of an Epochal Idea. In G. Mitman, M. Armiero and R. S. Emmett, eds., *Future Remains. A Cabinet of Curiosities for the Anthropocene*, Chicago: Chicago University Press, pp. 1–18.

Norgaard, R. B. (2013). The Econocene and the Delta. *San Francisco Estuary and Watershed Science*, **11**(3). http://doi.org/10.15447/sfews.2013v11is s3art9 Retrieved from https://escholarship.org/uc/item/4h98t2m0.

Orlandini, G. (2018–19). *A ferro e fango. L'estrattivismo, il disastro di Mariana e il Brasile nell'Antropocene* (Ph.D. Thesis), Università degli Studi di Napoli "L'Orientale," Napoli.

Parikka, J. (2015). *Anthrobscene*, Minneapolis: University of Minnesota Press.

Past, E. (2013). "Trash Is Gold": Documenting the Ecomafia and Campania's Waste Crisis. *Interdisciplinary Studies in Literature and Environment*, **20**(3), 597–621. DOI 10.1093/isle/ist075.

Patel, J., Nielsen, F.B.H., Badiani, A.A., et al. (2020). "Poverty, Inequality & COVID-19: The Forgotten Vulnerable," *Public Health*, **183**(2020):110-111, available online at www.ncbi.nlm.nih.gov/pmc/articles/PMC7221360/. http://doi.org/10.1016/j.puhe.2020.05.006.

Pellow, D. N. (2002). *Garbage Wars: The Struggle for Environmental jJustice in Chicago*, Cambridge (MA): The MIT Press.

Petricca, C., Moloo, Z., and Stoisser, M. (2020). *Hazardous e-waste recycling in Agbogbloshie, Accra, Ghana*, https://ejatlas.org/conflict/agbogbloshie-e-waste-landfill-ghana.

Pezzullo, P. C. (2003). Touring "Cancer Alley," Louisiana: performances of community and memory for environmental justice. *Text and Performance Quarterly*, **23**(3), 226–252. http://doi.org/10.1080/10462930310001635295.

Pianura Trial 2011a). Trial against Fiume et al., hearing of 10 January 2011, testimony of Marco Nonno.

Pianura Trial (2011b). Trial against Fiume et al., hearing of 10 January 2011, testimony of Luigi Bruno.

Pinto, A. & Pratas, R. (2017). Antonio e Rosa Maria from ADACE in Aveiro, www.toxicbios.eu/#/stories.

Provincia di Napoli (2008). Area ambiente, Direzione Tutela del Suolo, Richiesta dati relativi alla discarica Difrabi, località Pianura, Prot. 383–15/05/2008.

Pulido, L. (2019). Racism and the Anthropocene. In G. Mitman, M. Armiero and R. S. Emmett, eds., *Future Remains. A Cabinet of Curiosities for the Anthropocene*, Chicago: Chicago University Press, pp. 116–128.

Radio onda D'Urto (2010). Pratiche, 23 May 2020, podcast availabc at https://parole.radiondadurto.org/2020/05/23/puntata-14-pratiche/.

Raworth, K. (2014). Must the Anthropocene be a Manthropocene? *The Guardian* Mon 20 Oct 2014 www.theguardian.com/commentisfree/2014/oct/20/anthropocene-working-group-science-gender-bias.

Rockström, J., Steffen, W., Noone, K., et al. (2009). A safe operating space for humanity. *Nature*, **461**(7263), 472–475. http://doi.org/10.1038/461472a.

Rodrigues, D. E., Corradi Cruz, M.A., de Melo Dias, A.P. et al. (2016). Algumas análises sobre os impactos à saúde do desastre em Mariana (MG). In B. Milanez & C. Losekann, eds., *Desastre no Vale do Rio Doce: Antecedentes, impactos e ações sobre a destruição*, Rio De Janeiro: Folio Digital, pp. 163–193.

Roy, A. (2020), The pandemic is a portal, *Financial Times* 3 April 2020 www.ft.com/content/10d8f5e8-74eb-11ea-95fe-fcd274e920ca.

Roy, A. (1999). The Greater Common Good. *Frontline*, **16**(11) May 22 – June 04.

Samson, M. (2009). Movimento Nacional dos Catadores de Materiais Recicláveis (MNCR), Brazil. In M. Samson, ed., *Refusing To Be Cast Aside: Waste Pickers Organising Around The World*, Cambridge (MA): Women in Informal Employment: Globalizing and Organizing (WIEGO), pp. 40–49.

Samson, M. (2009). Wasted citizenship? Reclaimers and the privatised expansion of the public sphere. *Africa Development*, **XXXIV**(3 & 4), 1–25. http://doi.org/10.1177%2F0263775815600058.

Sarli, D. (2014). Da Posillipo a Pianura solo andata. In M. Armiero, ed., *Teresa e le altre. Storie di donne nella Terra dei Fuochi*, Milano: Jaca Book, pp. 101–112.

Scanlan, J. (2005). *On Garbage*, London: Reaktion Books.

Sebiorec (2010). Studio epidemiologico sullo stato di salute e sui livelli d'accumulo di contaminanti organici persistenti nel sangue e nel latte materno in gruppi di popolazione a differente rischio d'esposizione nella Regione Campania, 2010, availabe at http://speciali.espresso.repubblica.it/pdf/sebiorec2010.pdf.

Serao, M. (1884). *Il ventre di Napoli*, Milano: Treves.

Shah, M., Sachdeva, M., Dodiuk-Gad, R.P., (2020). COVID-19 and racial disparities. *Journal of the American Academy of Dermatology*, **83**(1), e35. http://doi.org/10.1016/j.jaad.2020.04.046.

Šehabović, Š, Gaknič, M., and Arsenijevic, D. (2020), *Zemlja-Voda-Zrak*, Sarajevo: Muzej knjizevnosti i pozorisne umjetnosti Bosne i Hercegovine.

Snowden, F. (1995). *Naples in the Time of Cholera, 1884–1911*, Cambridge (MA): Cambridge University Press.

Sofia Blu (2020). Interview in possession of the author.

Sofri, A. (2013). Il referendum di Taranto, *La Repubblica* 10/04/2013, retrieved from https://triskel182.wordpress.com/2013/04/10/il-referendum-di-taranto-adriano-sofri/.

Solnit, R. (2008). *Storming the Gates of Paradise: Landscapes for Politics*. Berkeley: University of California Press.

Solnit, R. (2009). *A Paradise Built in Hell: The Extraordinary Cmmunities that Arise in Disaster*, New York: Penguin Books.

Solórzano, D. G. & Yosso, T. J. (2002). Critical race methodology: Counter-storytelling as an analytical framework for education research. *Qualitative Inquiry*, **8**(1), 23–44. http://doi.org/10.1177/107780040200800103.

Strasser, S. (2013). *Waste and Want: A Social History of Trash*, New York: Henry Holt and Co.

Taylor (1999). *Making Salmon: An Environmental History of the Northwest Fisheries Crisis*, Seattle: University of Washington Press.

Tola, M. (2019). The archive and the lake: Labor, toxicity, and the making of cosmopolitical commons in Rome, Italy. *Environmental Humanities*, **11**(1): 194–215. https://doi.org/10.1215/22011919-7349499.

Tsing, A. L. (2015). *The Mushroom at the End of the World: On the Possibility of Life in Capitalist Ruins*. Princeton: Princeton University Press.

Tsing, A. L, Swanson, H. A., Gan, E., Bubandt, N., eds. (2017). *Arts of Living on a Damaged Planet: Ghosts and Monsters of the Anthropocene*, Minneapolis: University of Minnesota Press.

Tuncak, B. (2019). Report of the Special Rapporteur on the implications for human rights of the environmentally sound management and disposal of hazardous substances and wastes Seventy-fourth session Agenda item 70 (b) United Nation General Assembly Distr.: General 7 October 2019.

Valisena, D. (2020), *Coal lives: Italians and the metabolism of coal in Wallonia*, Belgium, *1945–1980*, (Ph.D. dissertation), KTH Royal Institute of Technology, Stockholm. urn: nbn:se:kth:diva-273012.

Vastano, L. (2008). *Vajont l'onda lunga, Firenze*: Ponte delle Grazie.

Vastano, L. (2017). Intervista a Carolina, multimedia project ToxicBios.eu.

Vecchio, B. (1974). *Il bosco negli scrittori italiani del Settecento e dell'età napoleonica*, Torino: Einaudi.

Verdicchio, P. (2016). Toxic Disorder and Civic Possibility: Viewing the Land of Fires from the Phlegraean Fields. In P. Verdicchio, ed., *Ecocritical Approaches to Italian Culture and Literature*, Lanham: Lexington Books.

Walker, L. Jardim, J. and Harley, K., (2010). *Wasteland*, documentary, Brazil.

White Mario, J. (1877). *La miseria di Napoli*, Firenze: Le Monnier.

Wu Ming (2013). *Storie #notav. Un anno e mezzo nella vita di Marco Bruno*, 2013 www.wumingfoundation.com/giap/2013/07/storie-notav-un-anno-e-mezzo-nella-vita-di-marco-bruno/.

Zhouri, A., Houri, A., Oliveira, R., Zucarelli, M., and Vasconcelos, M. (2017). The Rio Doce mining disaster in Brazil: between policies of reparation and the politics of affectations. *Vibrant, Virtual Braz. Anthr.*, **14**(2), e142081. http://doi.org/10.1590/1809-43412017v14n2p081.

Acknowledgements

This publication results from financial support from FORMAS (Swedish Research Council for Sustainable Development) under the National Research Programme on Climate (Contract: 2017–01962_3).

To the StopBiocidio activists
who have never surrendered to the Wasteocene

About the Author

Marco Armiero is the director of the KTH Environmental Humanities Laboratory and current president of the European Society for Environmental History. He has worked on the nationalization of nature, migrations and environment, and environmental justice. With his research, he has contributed to bridging environmental humanities and political ecology. Armiero also holds a position as Research Director at the CNR ISMed, in Italy.

Cambridge Elements $\equiv$

Environmental Humanities

Louise Westling
University of Oregon

Louise Westling is an American scholar of literature and environmental humanities who was a founding member of the Association for the Study of Literature and Environment and its President in 1998. She has been active in the international movement for environmental cultural studies, teaching and writing on landscape imagery in literature, critical animal studies, biosemiotics, phenomenology, and deep history.

Serenella Iovino
University of North Carolina at Chapel Hill

Serenella Iovino is Professor of Italian Studies and Environmental Humanities at the University of North Carolina at Chapel Hill. She has written on a wide range of topics, including environmental ethics and ecocritical theory, bioregionalism and landscape stu- dies, ecofeminism and posthumanism, comparative literature, eco-art, and the Anthropocene.

Timo Maran
University of Tartu

Timo Maran is an Estonian semiotician and poet. Maran is Professor of Ecosemiotics and Environmental Humanities and Head of the Department of Semiotics at the University of Tartu. His research interests are semiotic relations of nature and culture, Estonian nature writing, zoosemiotics and species conservation, semiotics of biological mimicry.

About the Series

The environmental humanities is a new transdisciplinary complex of approaches to the embeddedness of human life and culture in all the dynamics that characterize the life of the planet. These approaches reexamine our species' history in light of the intensifying awareness of drastic climate change and ongoing mass extinction. To engage this reality, Cambridge Elements in Environmental Humanities builds on the idea of a more hybrid and participatory mode of research and debate, connecting critical and creative fields.

Cambridge Elements ☰

Environmental Humanities

Elements in the Series

A full series listing is available at: www.cambridge.org/EIEH

Printed in the United States
by Baker & Taylor Publisher Services

Printed in the United States
by Baker & Taylor Publisher Services